THE SPIRIT-FILLED FATHER'S GUIDE TO TOTAL VICTORY

THE SPIRIT-FILLED FATHER'S GUIDE TO TOTAL VICTORY

Harrison House, Inc.
Tulsa, Oklahoma

The Spirit-Filled Father's Guide
to Total Victory
ISBN 0-89274-775-7
Copyright © 1994 by
Harrison House, Inc.
P. O. Box 35035
Tulsa, OK 74153

Published by Harrison House, Inc.
P. O. Box 35035
Tulsa, OK 74153

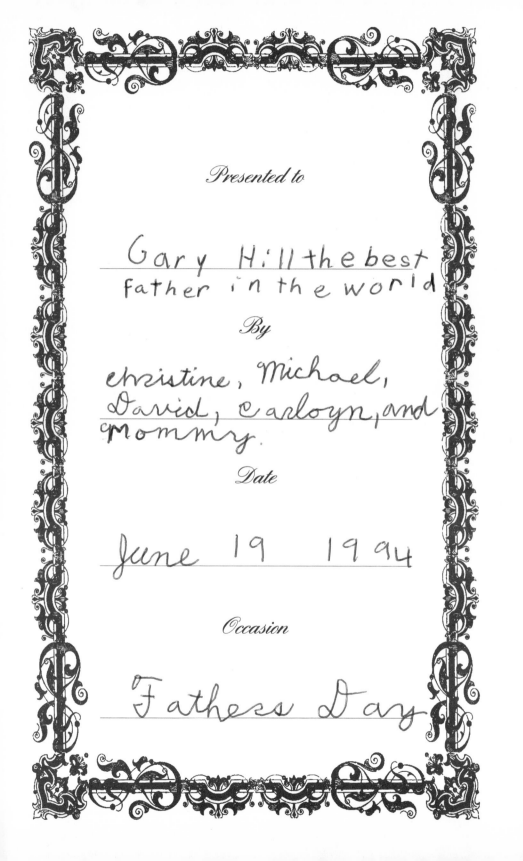

Presented to

Gary Hill the best
father in th e world

By

christine, Michael,
David, carloyn, and
mommy.

Date

June 19   19 94

Occasion

Fathers Day

"Be all the man God wants you to be — doctor, lawyer, gas station attendant, missionary, pastor, legislator, zoo keeper or whatever. Determine to live up to the potential that is within you, placed there by God."

Edwin Louis Cole

Contents

"Men of purpose change the world. World revival cannot come about by compromise, but only by people who know their God and know their calling and refuse to compromise with the devil or the world."

Lester Sumrall

YOUR PERSONAL RELATIONSHIP
WITH GOD

THE SALVATION EXPERIENCE

There Are Three Basic Reasons To Believe the Bible Is the Infallible and Pure Word of God

1. NO HUMAN WOULD HAVE WRITTEN A STANDARD THIS HIGH.
Think of the best person you know. You must admit he would have left certain scriptures out had he written the Bible. So the Bible projects an inhuman standard and way of life. It has to be God because no man you know would have ever written a standard that high.

2. THERE IS AN AURA, A CLIMATE, A CHARISMA, A PRESENCE THE BIBLE GENERATES WHICH NO OTHER BOOK IN THE WORLD CREATES.
Lay an encyclopedia on your table at the restaurant, nobody will look at you twice. But when you lay your Bible on the table, they will stare at you, watch you chew your food, and even read your license plate when you get in your car! Why? The Bible creates the presence of God and forces a reaction in the hearts of men.

3. THE NATURE OF MAN IS CHANGED WHEN HE READS THE BIBLE.
Men change. *Peace* enters into their spirits. Joy wells up within their lives. Men like what they become when they read this book. Men accept Christ, because this Bible says Jesus Christ is the Son of God and that all have sinned and the wages of sin will bring death; and the only forgiveness that they can find is through Jesus, the Son of God.

Three Basic Reasons for Accepting Christ

1. YOU NEEDED FORGIVENESS. At some point in your life, you will want to be clean. You will hate guilt; you will crave purity. You have a built-in desire toward God, and you will have to address that appetite at some point in your life.

2. YOU NEED A FRIEND. You may be sitting there saying, "But, don't I have friends?" Yes, but you have never had a friend like Jesus. Nobody can handle the information about your life as well as He can. He is the most consistent relationship you will ever know. Human friends vacillate in their reaction, depending on your mood or theirs. Jesus Christ never changes His opinion of you. Nobody can tell Him anything which will change His mind about you. You cannot enjoy His world without His companionship.

3. YOU NEEDED A FUTURE. All men have a built-in need for immortality, a craving for an eternity. God placed it within us. D. L. Moody once made a statement, "One of these days you are going to hear that I'm dead and gone. When you do, don't believe a word of it. I'll be more alive then, than at any other time in my life." Each of us wonders about eternity. What is death like? What happens when I die? Is there a hell? a heaven? a God? a devil? What happens? Every man wants to be around tomorrow. The only guarantee you will have of a future is to have the Eternal One on the inside of you. *He is Jesus Christ, the Son of God!*

The Gospel means Good News, you can change; your sins can be forgiven; your guilt can be dissolved; God loves *you*! He wants to be the difference in your life. **All have sinned, and come short of the glory of God** (Rom. 3:23, KJV). **The wages of sin is death** (Rom. 6:23, KJV). You might say, what does that mean? It means that all unconfessed sin will be judged and penalized, but that is not the end of the story. The second part of Romans 6:23 (KJV) says, **but the gift of God is eternal life through Jesus Christ our Lord.** What does that mean? It means that between the wrath and judgment of God upon your sin, Jesus Christ the Son of God stepped in and absorbed your judgment and your penalty for you. God says if you recognize and respect Him and His worth as the Son of God, judgment will be withheld, and you will receive a pardon, forgiveness of all your mistakes.

What do you have to do? If you believe in your heart that Jesus is the Son of God and that God raised Him from the dead on the third day, and confess that with your mouth, then you will be saved. (Rom. 10:9,10.) What does the word "saved" mean? *Removed from danger.* It simply means if you respect and recognize the worth of Jesus Christ, God will take you out of the danger zone and receive you as a child of the Most High God. What is His gift that you are to receive? His Son. **For God so loved the world, that he gave his only begotten Son, that whosoever believeth in him should not perish, but have everlasting life** (John 3:16, KJV). How do you accept His Son? Accept His mercy. How do you reject your sins? Confess them and turn away from them. If I confess my sins, he is faithful and just to forgive me my sins and to cleanse me from all unrighteousness. (1 John 1:9.) That is the Gospel.

Salvation Prayer

H eavenly Father, You have said in Your Word that anyone who confesses Your Son Jesus Christ as Lord and believes in his, or her, heart that You raised Him from the dead, will be saved.

I believe that Jesus is Your Son, Father, and I acknowledge that He gave His blood at Calvary to pay for my sin, sickness, poverty and spiritual death. I renounce every work of darkness, and I receive You now, Lord Jesus, as my personal Lord and Savior.

According to Your Word, Lord, I am now a new creation because I am "in Christ." My past is dead and gone, and I have new life in You. Thank You, Lord Jesus, for exchanging the unrighteousness in my life for Your righteousness. I am now the righteousness of God in You, Lord Jesus!

Scripture References:

Romans 10:9,10
2 Corinthians 5:17,21
Romans 6:23

1 Peter 2:24
Romans 3:23

How To Be Sure You Have Eternal Life Scriptures

I tell you the truth, whoever hears my word and believes him who sent me has eternal life and will not be condemned; he has crossed over from death to life.

John 5:24

I tell you the truth, he who believes has everlasting life.

John 6:47

Jesus said to her, "I am the resurrection and the life. He who believes in me will live, even though he dies;
"And whoever lives and believes in me will never die. Do you believe this?"

John 11:25,26

For my Father's will is that everyone who looks to the Son and believes in him shall have eternal life, and I will raise him up at the last day.

John 6:40

My sheep listen to my voice; I know them, and they follow me.
I give them eternal life, and they shall never perish; no one can snatch them out of my hand.

John 10:27,28

The man who loves his life will lose it, while the man who hates his life in this world will keep it for eternal life.

John 12:25

For you granted him authority over all people that he might give eternal life to all those you have given him.
Now this is eternal life: that they may know you, the only true God, and Jesus Christ, whom you have sent.

John 17:2,3

For the wages of sin is death, but the gift of God is eternal life in Christ Jesus our Lord.

Romans 6:23

And this is the testimony: God has given us eternal life, and this life is in his Son.

He who has the Son has life; he who does not have the Son of God does not have life.

I write these things to you who believe in the name of the Son of God so that you may know that you have eternal life.

1 John 5:11-13

RECEIVING THE INFILLING
OF THE HOLY SPIRIT

And I will pray the Father, and he shall give you another Comforter, that he may abide with you for ever; Even the Spirit of truth; whom the world cannot receive, because it seeth him not, neither knoweth him: but ye know him; for he dwelleth with you, and shall be in you.

John 14:16,17, KJV

Our Father has sent Someone to us, Someone Who will always be with us as Comforter and Guide. He has sent the Holy Spirit.

As a Christian, you have made a choice to follow God and commit yourself to His ways. He has given you the Holy Spirit to be with you as your direct link to Him. But you must receive the infilling of the Holy Spirit.

The Word of God sets only two requirements for receiving the infilling of the Holy Spirit: 1) experiencing the New Birth through Jesus Christ, and 2) asking to receive the baptism of the Holy Spirit.

And I say unto you, Ask, and it shall be given you; seek, and ye shall find; knock, and it shall be opened unto you. For every one that asketh receiveth; and he that seeketh findeth; and to him that knocketh it shall be opened. If a son shall ask bread of any of you that is a father, will he give him a stone? or if he ask a fish, will he for a fish give him a serpent? Or if he shall ask an egg, will he offer

him a scorpion? If ye then, being evil, know how to give good gifts unto your children: how much more shall your heavenly Father give the Holy Spirit to them that ask him?

Luke 11:9-13, KJV

If you have been born again as a Christian, accepting that Jesus became sin for your sins to be removed, then why should you, and how could you, cleanse yourself of any sin? You cannot cleanse yourself from sin; salvation is a free gift from God. In the same way, when you ask the Father for the Holy Spirit, He gives Him to you immediately. There is no certain manner of prayer or crying that you must perform; you just ask Him.

The Holy Spirit is a gift from the Father much like your salvation is a gift. He has given the Holy Spirit to you to draw you closer to Him for a more intimate relationship. He has also given the Holy Spirit to empower you with authority in this world.

And they were all filled with the Holy Ghost, and began to speak with other tongues, as the Spirit gave them utterance.

Acts 2:4, KJV

This clearly demonstrates what happens when you receive the infilling of the Holy Spirit with the evidence of speaking in tongues. Tongues is the Holy Spirit praying through you; not vocalizing for you, but giving you the words to speak. The language you speak is not your native language and is commonly referred to as tongues. There are wonderful benefits for praying daily in the Spirit. Praying in tongues stimulates your faith, enables you to pray for the unknown, edifies you and helps you pray in line with God's perfect will.

Realize that the Holy Spirit will give you words, but He is not going to pray for you. You will be doing the speaking with your tongue, your voice and your mouth. The Holy Spirit will bring the prompting, desire, or urge to speak. At first, it may be only a few syllables, but the more you pray, the more your language will develop.

If you do not speak in other tongues immediately, there are basically two things to check:

1) Did you sense an urging deep inside? That was the Holy Spirit prompting you. You just need to cooperate and respond by giving place to it. By faith, let the words form on your tongue.

2) If you did not sense the urging of the Holy Spirit inside you, then do not be concerned. We receive all things from God by faith, so you can educate yourself in faith by reading about the baptism of the Holy Spirit. (We recommend *Seven Vital Steps To Receiving the Holy Spirit* by Kenneth E. Hagin.) This will help you

to renew your mind and release any conscious or unconscious fear you may have had. The Bible says **faith cometh by hearing, and hearing by the word of God** (Rom. 10:17, KJV).

Infilling Prayer

Heavenly Father, I come to You in the name of Jesus to thank You because I am Your child. By faith I now receive the gift of the Holy Spirit, with the evidence of speaking in other tongues as the Holy Spirit gives me utterance.

As a Spirit-filled Christian, I am now empowered to be a victorious Christian and a bold witness of the Good News of Jesus Christ. Amen.

Scripture References:

John 14:16,17

Acts 1:8

Acts 2:38,39

Luke 11:13

Acts 2:4

Jude 20

$\Longrightarrow\!\!\times\!\!\Longleftarrow$

BEING FILLED WITH THE SPIRIT SCRIPTURES

But you will receive power when the Holy Spirit comes on you; and you will be my witnesses in Jerusalem, and in all Judea and Samaria, and to the ends of the earth.

Acts 1:8

Do not get drunk on wine, which leads to debauchery. Instead, be filled with the Spirit.

Ephesians 5:18

The Spirit of the Lord is on me, because he has anointed me to preach good news to the poor. He has sent me to proclaim freedom for the prisoners and recovery of sight for the blind, to release the oppressed.

Luke 4:18

From the west, men will fear the name of the Lord, and from the rising of the sun, they will revere his glory. For he will come like a pent-up flood that the breath of the Lord drives along.

Isaiah 59:19

"As for me, this is my covenant with them," says the Lord. "My Spirit, who is on you, and my words that I have put in your mouth will not depart from your mouth, or from the mouths of your children, or from the mouths of their descendants from this time on and forever," says the Lord.

Isaiah 59:21

The Spirit of the Sovereign Lord is on me, because the Lord has anointed me to preach good news to the poor. He has sent me to bind up the brokenhearted, to proclaim freedom for the captives and release from darkness for the prisoners.

Isaiah 61:1

My message and my preaching were not with wise and persuasive words, but with a demonstration of the Spirit's power.

1 Corinthians 2:4

And afterward, I will pour out my Spirit on all people. Your sons and daughters will prophesy, your old men will dream dreams, your young men will see visions.

Joel 2:28

I baptize you with water for repentance. But after me will come one who is more powerful than I, whose sandals I am not fit to carry. He will baptize you with the Holy Spirit and with fire.

Matthew 3:11

I am going to send you what my Father has promised; but stay in the city until you have been clothed with power from on high.

Luke 24:49

Suddenly a sound like the blowing of a violent wind came from heaven and filled the whole house where they were sitting.

They saw what seemed to be tongues of fire that separated and came to rest on each of them.

All of them were filled with the Holy Spirit and began to speak in other tongues as the Spirit enabled them.

Peter replied, "Repent and be baptized, every one of you, in the name of Jesus Christ for the forgiveness of your sins. And you will receive the gift of the Holy Spirit."

Acts 2:2-4,38

When they arrived, they prayed for them that they might receive the Holy Spirit,

Because the Holy Spirit had not yet come upon any of them; they had simply been baptized into the name of the Lord Jesus.

Then Peter and John placed their hands on them, and they received the Holy Spirit.

Acts 8:15-17

And the disciples were filled with joy and with the Holy Spirit.

Acts 13:52

And asked them, "Did you receive the Holy Spirit when you believed?" They answered, "No, we have not even heard that there is a Holy Spirit."

So Paul asked, "Then what baptism did you receive?" "John's baptism," they replied.

Paul said, "John's baptism was a baptism of repentance. He told the people to believe in the one coming after him, that is, in Jesus."

On hearing this, they were baptized into the name of the Lord Jesus.

When Paul placed his hands on them, the Holy Spirit came on them, and they spoke in tongues and prophesied.

Acts 19:2-6

May the God of hope fill you with all joy and peace as you trust in him, so that you may overflow with hope by the power of the Holy Spirit.

Romans 15:13

PRINCIPLES OF BIBLE STUDY

Nautical charts are used by sailors and maps are used by road travelers as their guidebooks and keys to their final destinations. Christians have a map and guidebook that is far superior to any other in the world – the Bible. This book is not just a great piece of literature; it is the main ingredient to a successful Christian life. The Scriptures are the inspired Word of God. Second Timothy 3:16,17 (KJV) says:

All scripture is given by inspiration of God, and is profitable for doctrine, for reproof, for correction, for instruction in righteousness: That the man of God may be perfect, throughly furnished unto all good works.

It is obvious from this passage that the Lord gave us His Word for specific reasons: to confirm our beliefs, to set spiritual and moral guidelines, to give us godly inspiration and wisdom for our daily living, and to instruct us in the ways of our Father. We cannot draw these things from the Word of God without daily study.

There are many ways to study the Bible, each with its own merit. Here are a few principles that will help you study earnestly.

1. ALWAYS HAVE THE RIGHT ATTITUDE TOWARD STUDYING YOUR BIBLE. Approach your daily study with an open heart and mind. Be ready to accept what the Lord has to show you.

2. REALIZE THAT STUDYING YOUR BIBLE ISN'T ALWAYS EASY. Sometimes reading and studying are hard work. Make yourself be consistent and faithful to daily study, and be a diligent student of God's Word. A systematic approach to Bible study can help you overcome difficult periods in your study times.

3. KEEP A RECORD OF WHAT YOU HAVE LEARNED. Write down what the Lord reveals to you during your study times. This will help you put your new wisdom to practice and provide a permanent record for you to refer to when you need it.

4. SHARE WITH OTHERS WHAT YOU HAVE LEARNED. Often, if you are willing, the Lord will show you a key to a problem that someone else can use, too. His wisdom is too wonderful to be kept hidden. Encourage someone else by sharing with him how your study time has strengthened you.

5. YOUR STUDY TIME IS MEANT TO ADD TO WORSHIP AND TEACHING SERVICES, NOT REPLACE THEM. This is your private, personal time for you to learn what your Father has in store for you, but it is meant to augment your fellowship at church and other meetings with believers. Your personal study time is not meant to be your own source of fellowship with the Lord.

6. FIND A CONSISTENT TIME AND PLACE TO STUDY. For example, you might start with ten to fifteen minutes a day with an eventual goal of thirty minutes. Many people prefer to study in the mornings so that they can be receptive to God and His wisdom throughout the day. The key is to find what works for you.

7. BE IN AN ATTITUDE OF PRAYER WHILE YOU READ. Ask the Holy Spirit to be your guide through the Scriptures. The Holy Spirit was given to help you grow in relationship with the Father, and that includes Bible study!

PRAYER TO WALK IN THE WORD

ather, in the name of Jesus, I accept Your Word as my road map for a successful life. I accept Your Word as the stabilizing force in my life, for You said it is forever settled in heaven.

Thank You, Father, that You have personalized Your Word for me. Because it is my standard for integrity, my guide for spiritual and moral principles and my daily inspiration and source of wisdom, I will meditate upon Your Word day and night.

I will give Your Word first place in my life, Father, for to walk in Your Word is to walk in relationship and in fellowship with You, with Jesus Christ Your Son and with the Holy Spirit. To walk in Your Word is to walk in victory in this life.

Because I want to know You more, Lord, I will delight myself in Your Word continually. Amen.

Scripture References:

Psalm 119:89

Mark 13:31

Psalm 1:2

Joshua 1:8

Psalm 119:105

STUDYING GOD'S WORD SCRIPTURES

Do not let this Book of the Law depart from your mouth; meditate on it day and night, so that you may be careful to do everything written in it. Then you will be prosperous and successful.

Joshua 1:8

All Scripture is God-breathed and is useful for teaching, rebuking, correcting and training in righteousness.

2 Timothy 3:16

Heaven and earth will pass away, but my words will never pass away.

Mark 13:31

Jesus answered, "It is written: 'Man does not live on bread alone, but on every word that comes from the mouth of God.'"

Matthew 4:4

For the word of God is living and active. Sharper than any double-edged sword, it penetrates even to dividing soul and spirit, joints and marrow; it judges the thoughts and attitudes of the heart.

Hebrews 4:12

For prophecy never had its origin in the will of man, but men spoke from God as they were carried along by the Holy Spirit.

2 Peter 1:21

But his delight is in the law of the Lord, and on his law he meditates day and night.

Psalm 1:2

Your word is a lamp to my feet and a light for my path.

Psalm 119:105

In God, whose word I praise, in God I trust; I will not be afraid. What can mortal man do to me?

Psalm 56:4

For everything that was written in the past was written to teach us, so that through endurance and the encouragement of the Scriptures we might have hope.

Romans 15:4

The grass withers and the flowers fall, but the word of our God stands forever.

Isaiah 40:8

He sent forth his word and healed them; he rescued them from the grave.

Psalm 107:20

Like newborn babies, crave pure spiritual milk, so that by it you may grow up in your salvation.

1 Peter 2:2

Do not merely listen to the word, and so deceive yourselves. Do what it says.

James 1:22

To the Jews who had believed him, Jesus said, "If you hold to my teaching, you are really my disciples.
"Then you will know the truth, and the truth will set you free."

John 8:31,32

Consequently, faith comes from hearing the message, and the message is heard through the word of Christ.

Romans 10:17

But the word of the Lord stands forever. And this is the word that was preached to you.

1 Peter 1:25

He remembers his covenant forever, the word he commanded, for a thousand generations.

1 Chronicles 16:15

So is my word that goes out from my mouth: It will not return to me empty, but will accomplish what I desire and achieve the purpose for which I sent it.

Isaiah 55:11

"IN-CHRIST" REALITIES

In Revelation 12:11, the Word says the saints overcame the accuser by the blood of Jesus and the *word of their testimony*. That is true not only for end-time martyrs, but it is true for born-again children of God living everyday lives in any generation.

However, you cannot have a "testimony" unless you know the "rights" of a born-again child of God, the things you inherited in, through, and with Jesus because of His work on the cross.

You must know who you are *in Christ*. Then, to bring those things *that you already possess* into manifestation, you must begin to believe them. To be born again, you must have faith that God exists and that He sent His only begotten Son to die for your sins because He loves you. (John 3:16.) Salvation is a free gift for you, purchased by Jesus, but unless you believe that and *confess* it with your mouth, salvation is not manifested in you. It is not a reality for you. (Rom. 10:9,10.)

First, find out from the Word what things are already yours because of Jesus. Then, if you want to build faith for those things to become real in your life, begin to speak out the good things God has done and the things you are believing for Him to do.

Faith without works is dead. (James 2:17.) Faith grows stronger by telling testimonies of Jesus, by continual confession of what you believe God will do.

A weak confession is one full of doubt and is a confession of defeat. As long as people talk defeat, they will not overcome. They have the blood of the Lamb, but the true "word of their testimony" is missing.

What *is* the confession, the word of our testimony, that we are told in Hebrews 4:14 to "hold fast"? It is the positive things God has done *in* our lives and *for* us. The word of our testimony is speaking out of who we are *in Christ*, not just what He has done for us in our natural lives.

From God's viewpoint, everything His Word says you are, or that you have, is true. Those things already are done! The Bible is a legal document setting forth the story, the description, and the provisions of the Blood Covenant, of which the Abrahamic Covenant (the Old Covenant) was a forerunner.

There are more than one hundred expressions such as "in Christ," "in Him," "in Whom," "through Whom," and so forth in the New Testament that set forth all the things Jesus provided for us by His blood on the cross of Calvary.

Start with Second Corinthians 5:17 (KJV):

Therefore if any man be *in Christ*, he is a new creature: old things are passed away; behold, all things are become new.

Then go on and memorize as many others as you can, confessing them often, so that the "word of your testimony" is in line with the Word of God. Finding out the reality of who you are *in Christ* will change your life!

PRAYER TO BE GOD-INSIDE MINDED

Father, You created me a three-part being: spirit, soul and body. My spirit, soul and body are nurtured daily with Your Word. Your Word strengthens my spirit, renews my mind, and brings control to my body, which is a temple of Your Spirit. I submit every area of my life to Your Word, Lord. You and Your Word are one.

Thank You, Holy Spirit, that You dominate my human spirit. I am led and controlled by Your Spirit in the daily affairs of life, Lord, rather than by my flesh.

I think good thoughts because Your Spirit dominates my mind, Lord, and my thoughts create in me a picture of who I am in You.

I am quick to obey Your voice, which causes me to triumph in every circumstance I face.

Scripture References:

1 Thessalonians 5:23	Romans 8:14,16
1 Corinthians 6:19,20	2 Corinthians 2:14
Proverbs 23:7	

KNOWING WHO YOU ARE IN CHRIST SCRIPTURES

No, in all these things we are more than conquerors through him who loved us.

Romans 8:37

For everyone born of God overcomes the world. This is the victory that has overcome the world, even our faith.

1 John 5:4

But thanks be to God, who always leads us in triumphal procession in Christ and through us spreads everywhere the fragrance of the knowledge of him.

2 Corinthians 2:14

But thanks be to God! He gives us the victory through our Lord Jesus Christ.

1 Corinthians 15:57

I can do everything through him who gives me strength.

Philippians 4:13

What, then, shall we say in response to this? If God is for us, who can be against us?

Romans 8:31

He replied, "Because you have so little faith. I tell you the truth, if you have faith as small as a mustard seed, you can say to this mountain, 'Move from here to there' and it will move. Nothing will be impossible for you."

Matthew 17:20

Jesus looked at them and said, "With man this is impossible, but with God all things are possible."

Matthew 19:26

For we are God's workmanship, created in Christ Jesus to do good works, which God prepared in advance for us to do.

Ephesians 2:10

I have been crucified with Christ and I no longer live, but Christ lives in me. The life I live in the body, I live by faith in the Son of God, who loved me and gave himself for me.

Galatians 2:20

Jesus looked at them and said, "With man this is impossible, but not with God; all things are possible with God."

Mark 10:27

For nothing is impossible with God.

Luke 1:37

Jesus replied, "What is impossible with men is possible with God."

Luke 18:27

Therefore, if anyone is in Christ, he is a new creation; the old has gone, the new has come!

2 Corinthians 5:17

God made him who had no sin to be sin for us, so that in him we might become the righteousness of God.

2 Corinthians 5:21

How great is the love the Father has lavished on us, that we should be called children of God! And that is what we are! The reason the world does not know us is that it did not know him.

Dear friends, now we are children of God, and what we will be has not yet been made known. But we know that when he appears, we shall be like him, for we shall see him as he is.

1 John 3:1,2

The Spirit himself testifies with our spirit that we are God's children.

Now if we are children, then we are heirs – heirs of God and co-heirs with Christ, if indeed we share in his sufferings in order that we may also share in his glory.

Romans 8:16,17

"For in him we live and move and have our being." As some of your own poets have said, "We are his offspring."

Acts 17:28

And God raised us up with Christ and seated us with him in the heavenly realms in Christ Jesus.

Ephesians 2:6

OTHER SCRIPTURES TO HELP YOU LIVE THE VICTORIOUS CHRISTIAN LIFE

DEVELOPING YOUR PRAYER LIFE

f you believe, you will receive whatever you ask for in prayer.

Matthew 21:22

Do not be anxious about anything, but in everything, by prayer and petition, with thanksgiving, present your requests to God.

Philippians 4:6

And the prayer offered in faith will make the sick person well; the Lord will raise him up. If he has sinned, he will be forgiven.

James 5:15

If my people, who are called by my name, will humble themselves and pray and seek my face and turn from their wicked ways, then will I hear from heaven and will forgive their sin and will heal their land.

2 Chronicles 7:14

Ask and it will be given to you; seek and you will find; knock and the door will be opened to you.

For everyone who asks receives; he who seeks finds; and to him who knocks, the door will be opened.

Matthew 7:7,8

I tell you the truth, if anyone says to this mountain, "Go, throw yourself into the sea," and does not doubt in his heart but believes that what he says will happen, it will be done for him.

Therefore I tell you, whatever you ask for in prayer, believe that you have received it, and it will be yours.

Mark 11:23,24

If you remain in me and my words remain in you, ask whatever you wish, and it will be given you.

John 15:7

Again, I tell you that if two of you on earth agree about anything you ask for, it will be done for you by my Father in heaven.

Matthew 18:19

And I will do whatever you ask in my name, so that the Son may bring glory to the Father.

You may ask me for anything in my name, and I will do it.

John 14:13,14

In that day you will no longer ask me anything. I tell you the truth, my Father will give you whatever you ask in my name.

Until now you have not asked for anything in my name. Ask and you will receive, and your joy will be complete.

John 16:23,24

But you, dear friends, build yourselves up in your most holy faith and pray in the Holy Spirit.

Jude 20

This is the confidence we have in approaching God: that if we ask anything according to his will, he hears us.

And if we know that he hears us – whatever we ask – we know that we have what we asked of him.

1 John 5:14,15

Let us then approach the throne of grace with confidence, so that we may receive mercy and find grace to help us in our time of need.

Hebrews 4:16

Therefore confess your sins to each other and pray for each other so that you may be healed. The prayer of a righteous man is powerful and effective.

James 5:16

The eyes of the Lord are on the righteous and his ears are attentive to their cry.

Psalm 34:15

Before they call I will answer; while they are still speaking I will hear.

Isaiah 65:24

Call to me and I will answer you and tell you great and unsearchable things you do not know.

Jeremiah 33:3

If you believe, you will receive whatever you ask for in prayer.

Matthew 21:22

I keep asking that the God of our Lord Jesus Christ, the glorious Father, may give you the Spirit of wisdom and revelation, so that you may know him better.

I pray also that the eyes of your heart may be enlightened in order that you may know the hope to which he has called you, the riches of his glorious inheritance in the saints,

And his incomparably great power for us who believe. That power is like the working of his mighty strength,

Which he exerted in Christ when he raised him from the dead and seated him at his right hand in the heavenly realms,

Far above all rule and authority, power and dominion, and every title that can be given, not only in the present age but also in the one to come.

And God placed all things under his feet and appointed him to be head over everything for the church,

Which is his body, the fullness of him who fills everything in every way.

Ephesians 1:17-23

For this reason I kneel before the Father,
From whom his whole family in heaven and on earth derives its name.

I pray that out of his glorious riches he may strengthen you with power through his Spirit in your inner being,

So that Christ may dwell in your hearts through faith. And I pray that you, being rooted and established in love,

May have power, together with all the saints, to grasp how wide and long and high and deep is the love of Christ,

And to know this love that surpasses knowledge – that you may be filled to the measure of all the fullness of God.

Now to him who is able to do immeasurably more than all we ask or imagine, according to his power that is at work within us,

To him be glory in the church and in Christ Jesus throughout all generations, for ever and ever! Amen.

Ephesians 3:14-21

And pray in the Spirit on all occasions with all kinds of prayers and requests. With this in mind, be alert and always keep on praying for all the saints.

Pray also for me, that whenever I open my mouth, words may be given me so that I will fearlessly make known the mystery of the gospel,

For which I am an ambassador in chains. Pray that I may declare it fearlessly, as I should.

Ephesians 6:18-20

For this reason, since the day we heard about you, we have not stopped praying for you and asking God to fill you with the knowledge of his will through all spiritual wisdom and understanding.

And we pray this in order that you may live a life worthy of the Lord and may please him in every way: bearing fruit in every good work, growing in the knowledge of God,

Being strengthened with all power according to his glorious might so that you may have great endurance and patience, and joyfully

Giving thanks to the Father, who has qualified you to share in the inheritance of the saints in the kingdom of light.

For he has rescued us from the dominion of darkness and brought us into the kingdom of the Son he loves,

In whom we have redemption, the forgiveness of sins.

Colossians 1:9-14

May the God of peace, who through the blood of the eternal covenant brought back from the dead our Lord Jesus, that great Shepherd of the sheep,

Equip you with everything good for doing his will, and may he work in us what is pleasing to him, through Jesus Christ, to whom be glory for ever and ever. Amen.

Hebrews 13:20,21

PRAISING AND WORSHIPPING GOD

They were also to stand every morning to thank and praise the Lord. They were to do the same in the evening.

1 Chronicles 23:30

The Lord is my strength and my shield; my heart trusts in him, and I am helped. My heart leaps for joy and I will give thanks to him in song.

Psalm 28:7

I will extol the Lord at all times; his praise will always be on my lips.

Psalm 34:1

Then we your people, the sheep of your pasture, will praise you forever; from generation to generation we will recount your praise.

Psalm 79:13

It is good to praise the Lord and make music to your name, O Most High, To proclaim your love in the morning and your faithfulness at night.

Psalm 92:1,2

O Lord, you are my God; I will exalt you and praise your name, for in perfect faithfulness you have done marvelous things, things planned long ago.

Isaiah 25:1

I will praise the Lord all my life; I will sing praise to my God as long as I live.

Psalm 146:2

Ascribe to the Lord the glory due his name; worship the Lord in the splendor of his holiness.

Psalm 29:2

Come, let us bow down in worship, let us kneel before the Lord our Maker.

Psalm 95:6

Yet a time is coming and has now come when the true worshipers will worship the Father in spirit and truth, for they are the kind of worshipers the Father seeks.

God is spirit, and his worshipers must worship in spirit and in truth.

John 4:23,24

I praise you because I am fearfully and wonderfully made; your works are wonderful, I know that full well.

Psalm 139:14

From birth I have relied on you; you brought me forth from my mother's womb. I will ever praise you.

Psalm 71:6

My tongue will speak of your righteousness and of your praises all day long.

Psalm 35:28

OBEDIENCE

If you are willing and obedient, you will eat the best from the land.

Isaiah 1:19

All the ways of the Lord are loving and faithful for those who keep the demands of his covenant.

Psalm 25:10

The fear of the Lord is the beginning of wisdom; all who follow his precepts have good understanding. To him belongs eternal praise.

Psalm 111:10

Teach me to do your will, for you are my God; may your good Spirit lead me on level ground.

Psalm 143:10

For whoever does the will of my Father in heaven is my brother and sister and mother.

Matthew 12:50

Peter and the other apostles replied: "We must obey God rather than men!"

Acts 5:29

This is how we know that we love the children of God: by loving God and carrying out his commands.

This is the love for God: to obey his commands. And his commands are not burdensome.

1 John 5:2,3

And the people said to Joshua, "We will serve the Lord our God and obey him."

Joshua 24:24

Now if you obey me fully and keep my covenant, then out of all nations you will be my treasured possession.

Exodus 19:5a

If you love me, you will obey what I command.

John 14:15

UNDERSTANDING YOUR AUTHORITY OVER THE DEVIL

And these signs will accompany those who believe: In my name they will drive out demons; they will speak in new tongues.

Mark 16:17

And do not give the devil a foothold.

Ephesians 4:27

Finally, be strong in the Lord and in his mighty power.

Put on the full armor of God so that you can take your stand against the devil's schemes.

For our struggle is not against flesh and blood, but against the rulers, against the authorities, against the powers of this dark world and against the spiritual forces of evil in the heavenly realms.

Therefore put on the full armor of God, so that when the day of evil comes, you may be able to stand your ground, and after you have done everything, to stand.

Stand firm then, with the belt of truth buckled around your waist, with the breastplate of righteousness in place,

And with your feet fitted with the readiness that comes from the gospel of peace.

In addition to all this, take up the shield of faith, with which you can extinguish all the flaming arrows of the evil one.

Take the helmet of salvation and the sword of the Spirit, which is the word of God.

And pray in the Spirit on all occasions with all kinds of prayers and requests. With this in mind, be alert and always keep on praying for all the saints.

Ephesians 6:10-18

For though we live in the world, we do not wage war as the world does.

The weapons we fight with are not the weapons of the world. On the contrary, they have divine power to demolish strongholds.

We demolish arguments and every pretension that sets itself up against the knowledge of God, and we take captive every thought to make it obedient to Christ.

2 Corinthians 10:3-5

The Lord will rescue me from every evil attack and will bring me safely to his heavenly kingdom. To him be glory for ever and ever. Amen.

2 Timothy 4:18

If this is so, then the Lord knows how to rescue godly men from trials and to hold the unrighteous for the day of judgment, while continuing their punishment.

2 Peter 2:9

Be self-controlled and alert. Your enemy the devil prowls around like a roaring lion looking for someone to devour.

1 Peter 5:8

Submit yourselves, then, to God. Resist the devil, and he will flee from you.

James 4:7

How God anointed Jesus of Nazareth with the Holy Spirit and power, and how he went around doing good and healing all who were under the power of the devil, because God was with him.

Acts 10:38

When Jesus had called the Twelve together, he gave them power and authority to drive out all demons and to cure diseases.

Luke 9:1

I have given you authority to trample on snakes and scorpions and to overcome all the power of the enemy; nothing will harm you.

Luke 10:19

As for you, you were dead in your transgressions and sins,

In which you used to live when you followed the ways of this world and of the ruler of the kingdom of the air, the spirit who is now at work in those who are disobedient.

All of us also lived among them at one time, gratifying the cravings of our sinful nature and following its desires and thoughts. Like the rest, we were by nature objects of wrath.

But because of his great love for us, God, who is rich in mercy,

Made us alive with Christ even when we were dead in transgressions – it is by grace you have been saved.

And God raised us up with Christ and seated us with him in the heavenly realms in Christ Jesus.

Ephesians 2:1-6

"The greatest reward a man could ever hope to receive this side of eternity, is to see his children cherishing the faith which he entrusted to them. And to watch with thanksgiving as they make the family's spiritual tradition their own and a vital part of their children's lives."

Richard Exley

SPIRITUAL LEADERSHIP
IN THE HOME

"MEN TAKING THE SPIRITUAL LEADERSHIP IN THE HOME"

BY BILLY JOE DAUGHERTY

When men are in proper relationship to Jesus, they will rise up to be the spiritual leaders in their homes. They will have the spiritual strength they need, and they will have the Word of God to guide them.

Whether the family goes to church or not shouldn't be the wife's decision. It should be the man who says, "We're going to attend church." Men are responsible to set the example of what's important in the family.

Men should set the example in Bible reading in the home. It shouldn't be only at Christmas time that they read the Bible to their family. Thank God that it is done then, but it needs to happen more than once a year. Reading the Word will bring light into the home.

I would like to challenge men to spend as much time reading the Bible in the family as they do reading the newspaper. People often say, "We don't have time." How much time is spent watching television? How much time is spent reading periodicals? How much time is spent reading the newspaper? There's time to read the Bible, but it's a matter of priority.

It's not only the family who prays together who stays together, but it's the family who receives the light of God's Word. Men are responsible, not only for getting the family in church and being the example in the home, but also for prayer in the family.

It's very humbling for men to say, "Let's pray together." It's good for the ego! It's good for men to call the family together and say, "Let's have our devotions together." We have four children and I'll admit, it's an event to get everyone together. Men are responsible for setting the example of what's priority in life.

Most of the problems we're facing in America go back to a default by Christian parents in raising their children in the nurture and admonition of the Lord. When parents don't train their children in the way they should go, in the next generation there's even more secularism and godlessness. We're called to raise a new standard of the Word of God and prayer in our homes.

Men should be the ones to see that goals are established for the family. Businessmen can chart what they're targeting for in the future. Likewise, we should chart that we're targeting to see our children serving God 25 years from now.

WHEN YOU WANT TO BE...

THE LOVING FATHER

Hatred stirs up dissension, but love covers over all wrongs.

Proverbs 10:12

He who spares the rod hates his son, but he who loves him is careful to discipline him.

Proverbs 13:24

A new command I give you: Love one another. As I have loved you, so you must love one another.

By this all men will know that you are my disciples, if you love one another.

John 13:34,35

As the Father has loved me, so have I loved you. Now remain in my love.

If you obey my commands, you will remain in my love, just as I have obeyed my Father's commands and remain in his love.

My command is this: Love each other as I have loved you.

Greater love has no one than this, that he lay down his life for his friends.

You are my friends if you do what I command.

This is my command: Love each other.

John 15:9,10,12-14,17

Let no debt remain outstanding, except the continuing debt to love one another, for he who loves his fellowman has fulfilled the law.

Love does no harm to its neighbor. Therefore love is the fulfillment of the law.

Romans 13:8,10

If I speak in the tongues of men and of angels, but have not love, I am only a resounding gong or a clanging cymbal.

If I have the gift of prophecy and can fathom all mysteries and all knowledge, and if I have a faith that can move mountains, but have not love, I am nothing.

If I give all I possess to the poor and surrender my body to the flames, but have not love, I gain nothing.

Love is patient, love is kind. It does not envy, it does not boast, it is not proud.

It is not rude, it is not self-seeking, it is not easily angered, it keeps no record of wrongs.

It always protects, always trusts, always hopes, always perseveres.

Love never fails.

1 Corinthians 13:1-5,7,8a

And now these three remain: faith, hope and love. But the greatest of these is love.

1 Corinthians 13:13

Each one should test his own actions. Then he can take pride in himself, without comparing himself to somebody else.

Galatians 6:4

This is the message you heard from the beginning: We should love one another.

We know that we have passed from death to life, because we love our brothers. Anyone who does not love remains in death.

Dear children, let us not love with words or tongue but with actions and in truth.

1 John 3:11,14,18

Dear friends, let us love one another, for love comes from God. Everyone who loves has been born of God and knows God.

Whoever does not love does not know God, because God is love.

1 John 4:7,8

THE UNDERSTANDING FATHER

will praise the Lord, who counsels me; even at night my heart instructs me.
Psalm 16:7

As for God, his way is perfect; the word of the Lord is flawless. He is a shield for all who take refuge in him.
Psalm 18:30

Teach me your way, O Lord; lead me in a straight path because of my oppressors.
Psalm 27:11

Send forth your light and your truth, let them guide me; let them bring me to your holy mountain, to the place where you dwell.
Psalm 43:3

The Lord will fulfill his purpose for me; your love, O Lord, endures forever — do not abandon the works of your hands.
Psalm 138:8

Trust in the Lord with all your heart and lean not on your own understanding; in all your ways acknowledge him, and he will make your paths straight.
Proverbs 3:5,6

Counsel and sound judgment are mine; I have understanding and power.
Proverbs 8:14

Understanding is a fountain of life to those who have it, but folly brings punishment to fools.
A wise man's heart guides his mouth, and his lips promote instruction.
Proverbs 16:22,23

By wisdom a house is built, and through understanding it is established; through knowledge its rooms are filled with rare and beautiful treasures.
Proverbs 24:3,4

"For my thoughts are not your thoughts, neither are your ways my ways," declares the Lord.

"As the heavens are higher than the earth, so are my ways higher than your ways and my thoughts than your thoughts."

Isaiah 55:8,9

Call to me and I will answer you and tell you great and unsearchable things you do not know.

Jeremiah 33:3

THE PATIENT FATHER

But as for you, be strong and do not give up, for your work will be rewarded.
2 Chronicles 15:7

Wait for the Lord; be strong and take heart and wait for the Lord.
Psalm 27:14

Be still before the Lord and wait patiently for him; do not fret when men succeed in their ways, when they carry out their wicked schemes.
Psalm 37:7

I waited patiently for the Lord; he turned to me and heard my cry.
Psalm 40:1

For you have been my hope, O Sovereign Lord, my confidence since my youth.

Psalm 71:5

The end of a matter is better than its beginning, and patience is better than pride.

Do not be quickly provoked in your spirit, for anger resides in the lap of fools.
Ecclesiastes 7:8,9

But those who hope in the Lord will renew their strength. They will soar on wings like eagles; they will run and not grow weary, they will walk and not be faint.
Isaiah 40:31

But blessed is the man who trusts in the Lord, whose confidence is in him.

Jeremiah 17:7

And not only so, but we glory in tribulations also: knowing that tribulation worketh patience;

And patience, experience; and experience, hope:

And hope maketh not ashamed; because the love of God is shed abroad in our hearts by the Holy Ghost which is given unto us.

Romans 5:3-5, KJV

But if we hope for what we do not yet have, we wait for it patiently.

Romans 8:25

For everything that was written in the past was written to teach us, so that through endurance and the encouragement of the Scriptures we might have hope.

May the God who gives endurance and encouragement give you a spirit of unity among yourselves as you follow Christ Jesus.

May the God of hope fill you with all joy and peace as you trust in him, so that you may overflow with hope by the power of the Holy Spirit.

Romans 15:4,5,13

But the fruit of the Spirit is love, joy, peace, patience, kindness, goodness, faithfulness.

Galatians 5:22

I can do everything through him who gives me strength.

Philippians 4:13

We do not want you to become lazy, but to imitate those who through faith and patience inherit what has been promised.

Hebrews 6:12

So do not throw away your confidence; it will be richly rewarded.

You need to persevere so that when you have done the will of God, you will receive what he has promised.

For in just a very little while, He who is coming will come and will not delay.

Hebrews 10:35-37

Because you know that the testing of your faith develops perseverance. Perseverance must finish its work so that you may be mature and complete, not lacking anything.

James 1:3,4

✄

THE GODLY FATHER

He who walks with the wise grows wise, but a companion of fools suffers harm.

Proverbs 13:20

And if anyone gives even a cup of cold water to one of these little ones because he is my disciple, I tell you the truth, he will certainly not lose his reward.

Matthew 10:42

Just as the Son of Man did not come to be served, but to serve, and to give his life as a ransom for many.

Matthew 20:28

I tell you the truth, no servant is greater than his master, nor is a messenger greater than the one who sent him.

A new command I give you: Love one another. As I have loved you, so you must love one another.

John 13:16,34

May the God who gives endurance and encouragement give you a spirit of unity among yourselves as you follow Christ Jesus, so that with one heart and mouth you may glorify the God and Father of our Lord Jesus Christ.

Accept one another, then, just as Christ accepted you, in order to bring praise to God.

Romans 15:5-7

Now it is required that those who have been given a trust must prove faithful.

1 Corinthians 4:2

Therefore, my dear brothers, stand firm. Let nothing move you. Always give yourselves fully to the work of the Lord, because you know that your labor in the Lord is not in vain.

1 Corinthians 15:58

Carry each other's burdens, and in this way you will fulfill the law of Christ.
Therefore, as we have opportunity, let us do good to all people, especially to those who belong to the family of believers.

Galatians 6:2,10

Be imitators of God, therefore, as dearly loved children and live a life of love, just as Christ loved us and gave himself up for us as a fragrant offering and sacrifice to God.

Ephesians 5:1,2

Slaves, obey your earthly masters with respect and fear, and with sincerity of heart, just as you would obey Christ.
Serve wholeheartedly, as if you were serving the Lord, not men.

Ephesians 6:5,7

Your attitude should be the same as that of Christ Jesus:
Who, being in very nature God, did not consider equality with God something to be grasped, but made himself nothing, taking the very nature of a servant, being made in human likeness.
And being found in appearance as a man, he humbled himself and became obedient to death – even death on a cross!

Philippians 2:5-8

Bear with each other and forgive whatever grievances you may have against one another. Forgive as the Lord forgave you.
Slaves, obey your earthly masters in everything; and do it, not only when their eye is on you and to win their favor, but with sincerity of heart and reverence for the Lord.

Colossians 3:13,22

Let us fix our eyes on Jesus, the author and perfecter of our faith, who for the joy set before him endured the cross, scorning its shame, and sat down at the right hand of the throne of God.
Consider him who endured such opposition from sinful men, so that you will not grow weary and lose heart.

Hebrews 12:2,3

To this you were called, because Christ suffered for you, leaving you an example, that you should follow in his steps.

1 Peter 2:21

THE FATHER WHO IS A LEADER

As for you, if you walk before me in integrity of heart and uprightness, as David your father did, and do all I command and observe my decrees and laws, I will establish your royal throne over Israel forever, as I promised David your father when I said, "You shall never fail to have a man on the throne of Israel."

1 Kings 9:4,5

If the Lord delights in a man's way, he makes his steps firm.

Psalm 37:23

For the Lord God is a sun and shield; the Lord bestows favor and honor; no good thing does he withhold from those whose walk is blameless.

Psalm 84:11

Good will come to him who is generous and lends freely, who conducts his affairs with justice.

Psalm 112:5

Better a little with righteousness than much gain with injustice.
In his heart a man plans his course, but the Lord determines his steps.

Proverbs 16:8,9

Whether you turn to the right or to the left, your ears will hear a voice behind you, saying, "This is the way; walk in it."

Isaiah 30:21

This is what the Lord Almighty says: "Administer true justice; show mercy and compassion to one another.
"Do not oppress the widow or the fatherless, the alien or the poor. In your hearts do not think evil of each other."

Zechariah 7:9,10

For in the same way you judge others, you will be judged, and with the measure you use, it will be measured to you.

Matthew 7:2

But when he, the Spirit of truth, comes, he will guide you into all truth. He will not speak on his own; he will speak only what he hears, and he will tell you what is yet to come.

John 16:13

Because those who are led by the Spirit of God are sons of God.

Romans 8:14

I urge, then, first of all, that requests, prayers, intercession and thanksgiving be made for everyone –
For kings and all those in authority, that we may live peaceful and quiet lives in all godliness and holiness.

1 Timothy 2:1,2

Submit yourselves for the Lord's sake to every authority instituted among men: whether to the king, as the supreme authority,
Or to governors, who are sent by him to punish those who do wrong and to commend those who do right.
For it is God's will that by doing good you should silence the ignorant talk of foolish men.

1 Peter 2:13-15

THE PROVIDING FATHER

Since you are my rock and my fortress, for the sake of your name lead and guide me.

Psalm 31:3

Trust in the Lord and do good; dwell in the land and enjoy safe pasture.
Delight yourself in the Lord and he will give you the desires of your heart.
Commit your way to the Lord; trust in him and he will do this:
He will make your righteousness shine like the dawn, the justice of your cause like the noonday sun.
For evil men will be cut off, but those who hope in the Lord will inherit the land.
I was young and now I am old, yet I have never seen the righteous forsaken or their children begging bread.

For the Lord loves the just and will not forsake his faithful ones. They will be protected forever, but the offspring of the wicked will be cut off.

Psalm 37:3-6,9,25,28

You have been a refuge for the poor, a refuge for the needy in his distress, a shelter from the storm and a shade from the heat. For the breath of the ruthless is like a storm driving against a wall.

Isaiah 25:4

I can do everything through him who gives me strength.
And my God will meet all your needs according to his glorious riches in Christ Jesus.

Philippians 4:13,19

If any of you lacks wisdom, he should ask God, who gives generously to all without finding fault, and it will be given to him.

James 1:5

But the wisdom that comes from heaven is first of all pure; then peace-loving, considerate, submissive, full of mercy and good fruit, impartial and sincere.
Peacemakers who sow in peace raise a harvest of righteousness.

James 3:17,18

The prayer of a righteous man is powerful and effective.

James 5:16b

WHEN YOU FIND IT DIFFICULT TO BE THE SPIRITUAL LEADER IN YOUR HOME

That you may tell your children and grandchildren how I dealt harshly with the Egyptians and how I performed my signs among them, and that you may know that I am the Lord.

Exodus 10:2

On that day tell your son, "I do this because of what the Lord did for me when I came out of Egypt."

Exodus 13:8

Only be careful, and watch yourselves closely so that you do not forget the things your eyes have seen or let them slip from your heart as long as you live. Teach them to your children and to their children after them.

Deuteronomy 4:9

Counsel and sound judgment are mine; I have understanding and power.

Proverbs 8:14

So do not fear, for I am with you; do not be dismayed, for I am your God. I will strengthen you and help you; I will uphold you with my righteous right hand.

Isaiah 41:10

The Sovereign Lord is my strength; he makes my feet like the feet of a deer, he enables me to go on the heights.

Habakkuk 3:19a

But you will receive power when the Holy Spirit comes on you; and you will be my witnesses in Jerusalem, and in all Judea and Samaria, and to the ends of the earth.

Acts 1:8

Now to him who is able to do immeasurably more than all we ask or imagine, according to his power that is at work within us.

Ephesians 3:20

I can do everything through him who gives me strength.

Philippians 4:13

Being strengthened with all power according to his glorious might so that you may have great endurance and patience, and joyfully giving thanks to the Father, who has qualified you to share in the inheritance of the saints in the kingdom of light.

Colossians 1:11,12

So do not throw away your confidence; it will be richly rewarded.
You need to persevere so that when you have done the will of God, you will receive what he has promised.

Hebrews 10:35,36

"If you want to have a happy marriage, become your mate's best friend. Listen to one another. Nurture and care for each other. Every time you get together with your mate, it ought to be a privilege and a joy. Put a high value on the mate God has given you, and watch your marriage be like heaven on earth."

Mack & Brenda Timberlake

LOVING YOUR WIFE AS YOURSELF

"THE DUTIES OF A HUSBAND:
LOVE YOUR WIFE AS YOURSELF"
BY FREDERICK K. C. PRICE

I am a firm believer in the scriptural admonition that **the truth shall make you free** (John 8:32, KJV). The first truth I want to talk about here is found in Ephesians 5:25 (KJV):

Husbands, love your wives, even as...

That term, **even as**, is a prelude showing you how to do it. If you do not know how to love your wife, the Apostle Paul is getting ready to show you how. He is getting ready to give you an object lesson, one that you have to be deaf, dumb, blind, or dishonest not to see. He said:

Husbands, love your wives, even as Christ also loved the church, and gave himself for it.

So we see that the relationship of Jesus to the Church is the example for the relationship of the husband to the wife.

If we want to learn how to treat our wives, all we have to do is examine how Jesus treats the Church. There are Christian men, men filled with the Spirit, who do not know how to treat their wives. They are not treating their wives in a way or a manner that reflects love. They are surely not treating their wives as Christ treats the Church.

LOVE MEANS GIVING

Notice that Paul said, **even as Christ also loved the church, and gave himself for it.**

So love is giving of oneself to another. And in this context, it is the husband giving himself for his wife. That means *to* his wife and *for* his wife, because that is exactly what Jesus did. If you do give, obviously there will be some times of receiving. But your giving should not be based upon receiving. Giving should be a motive of the heart.

I am well persuaded that there are many Christian men who do not love their wives, because if they did, they would not treat them the way they do. The Word says **faith without works is dead** (James 2:20, KJV), and I have news for you: Love without works also is dead and meaningless. *Works* means "actions." I say many men do not love their wives, because the way they treat them is certainly not the way Christ treats us.

LOVE MEANS COMMUNICATION

Some husbands spend time talking to every woman on the job, then come home and will not talk to their wives. Anything Jesus had to say to the Church, He said in the Word. He instructed us. He told us that which would help and that which would be good. He did not hold it back from us.

I do not find where Jesus ever went off somewhere without telling the Church He was going, leaving us to wonder where He went and if He was coming back.

He said, "I am going, but I am coming again. You can count on it." (John 14:3.)

Jesus never mistreats the Church in any way. He sacrificed Himself for the Church. Jesus gave everything for us. He said:

Greater love hath no man than this, that a man lay down his life for his friends.

Ye are my friends, if ye do whatsoever I command you.

John 15:13,14, KJV

He gave Himself for us, as His "friends," and He still is giving Himself for us as High Priest for the Church.

An awful lot of Christian men are not giving anything to their wives – no time, no love, and no respect. They treat them like cattle. They treat them like a machine in the home, a machine to provide sex, wash dirty clothes, clean the house, take care of the children, and fix the meals. But that is about it. There is no real respect, no bringing her into the conversation.

Even the Lord said, **Come now, and let us reason together** (Is. 1:18, KJV). Many husbands do not discuss things with their wives. They just decide to do something and go ahead and do it.

"Well, I am the man, the head of the house, and I have always wanted a red Cadillac with white interior, so I'm going to go get one."

But the Word said that you and your wife are one. (Gen. 2:24.) Suppose she does not like a Cadillac? Especially a red one with a white interior. Does she not have a choice in the matter? She should, if she is one with you. Jesus never did that to the Church.

The Apostle Paul told us why Jesus gave Himself for the Church:

That he might sanctify and cleanse it with the washing of water by the word,

That he might present it to himself a glorious church, not having spot, or wrinkle, or any such thing; but that it should be holy and without blemish.

So ought men to love their wives as their own bodies. He that loveth his wife loveth himself.

Ephesians 5:26-28, KJV

Paul is saying that Jesus loved the Body and gave Himself for it. Then He relates the love of Jesus to how men should act and feel toward their wives. **So ought men to love their wives** (v. 28a). Men ought to love their wives in a self-sacrificing way, as they love their own bodies. That is how Jesus loves us, as His Body.

The opposite would be true, as well. If a man does not love himself, he cannot love his wife. Probably this is one reason why some people have such a difficult time loving other people. They really do not like themselves. Many people do not like themselves because they do not have a good self-image, although they put up a big smoke screen. Then they only like other people to the point that they can use them or get where they want to go.

Communication is a two-way street. It does not just mean telling her what you think. It means listening to what she thinks. It does not mean coming home and giving her a blow-by-blow description of your day, then picking up the paper or turning on the TV when she begins to tell you about hers.

Also, husbands who cannot receive revelation knowledge from their wives are in trouble! God can give you wisdom through anyone or anything He chooses. If you refuse to receive spiritual revelation, you are refusing God, not just your wife.

You are in this thing together, and whatever one gets is going to affect both of you. If you have a good wife who is willing to share what she gets in study and prayer with you, then you are crazy not to receive it. You do not have to feel less than a man because your wife came up with it. Be glad she did. Be glad somebody came up with it, because you surely had not! You should not feel inadequate. Perhaps she has a little more time during the day. I am glad when my wife comes up with good ideas, because I am affected in a positive way.

——➤✖◄——

LOVE MEANS SELF-SACRIFICE

Most men love themselves. I did not say *worship*. Nor did I say *idolize*. But I did say *love*. There is a difference.

The Pharisees (the religious leaders) were continually trying to entrap Jesus, and they came to Him one day and said, "What is the greatest commandment of all?" And He answered them this way:

...Thou shalt love the Lord thy God with all thy heart, and with all thy soul, and with all thy mind.

This is the first and great commandment.

And the second is like unto it, Thou shalt love thy neighbour as thyself.

On these two commandments hang all the law and the prophets.

Matthew 22:37-40, KJV

If you do not love yourself, you certainly cannot love your neighbor. Your neighbor is not just the person who lives next door to you. Your *neighbor* is everyone else in the world but you.

Paul said it very clearly, He who does not love his wife does not love himself. He who does not love himself does not love his wife.

Most men take care of themselves. Most men spend time on themselves.

Let me say it this way: I surely take care of me. I found out that "me" is somebody. Jesus made me somebody. He told me that I was a priest and a king, a member of a royal priesthood. He told me I was the head and not the tail, above and not beneath. He told me that Father God loved me so much He sent His only begotten Son to redeem me. I must be worth something. In the sight of God, I am. I bathe myself, shave, and put on cologne. I comb my hair. I buy good stuff to put on me, because I love myself and God loves me.

If that is true, then I cannot love my wife less than I love me. Yet some men never buy anything for their wives, never do anything for them.

Paul said in Ephesians 5:29 (KJV):

For no man ever yet hated his own flesh; but nourisheth and cherisheth it, even as the Lord the church.

Do you hate your own flesh? I have never seen a man ball up his fist, hit himself, and give himself a black eye. I have never seen that. But I have known of Christian men who gave their wives black eyes. Now, what kind of man is that? What kind of love is that? That is not the way Jesus does.

<hr>

LOVE YOUR WIFE WITH YOUR MONEY

This verse is saying the same thing: We are to love our wives as our own flesh. That means to take care of them. Some men spend more money on their cars than their wives. Some spend more on bowling balls or golf clubs than they do their wives. Some spend more on fishing equipment than wives.

I know some wives who do not even know where their husbands work. They do not know how much money they make. The husbands just come in and hand them some money, maybe enough to buy groceries or pay a couple of bills. That really gives those wives a sense of security, you know!

Betty knows every nickel and dime I get. If I find a dime on the sidewalk, she knows about it. Not because I have to let her know or because somebody has a gun at my head making me tell her. She is my *wife*. She is equal partner in this relationship. Whatever I go through, she has to go through. If the congregation blesses me or praises me, she gets blessed too. On the other hand, if the next day, the congregation says, "Crucify him! Away with him!" she is in on that too.

It is not fair for a man to treat his wife like she was a piece of furniture. In fact, some men have more respect for their furniture than their wives.

Men, you should treat your wives like queens. Then maybe they would begin to act like queens and begin to live like that. You know, if you get stepped on every day, it is hard not to act like a rug. As you relate to your wife, that is really the way you relate to Christ. Tell her that you love her and just talk things over with her. You know she is a part of you. She is *one* with you. She should be involved in everything you are involved with.

If you think she will not understand the kind of work you do, perhaps that is because you have never taken the time to explain it. Talk about the part that she can understand.

Betty and I talk about everything at the dinner table. Usually, we have not seen each other all day and perhaps have not had time to talk on the phone, so when I get home, I begin sharing my day with her. She is a part of my life. She is a part of the ministry.

And I always ask her what happened with her day. We talk and share. We keep one another posted on what is going on, because whatever affects one of us is going to affect the other. We take time to talk. She is bone of my bone and flesh of my flesh.

The main emphasis I want to make is how the Bible tells men to treat their wives.

One lady who had been married to the same man for thirty-two years wrote me a letter. She had always worked and helped her husband. Then in 1981, he closed out their checking accounts and refused to give her any money. He claimed their house and their money. She does not know where his savings account is. When his job requires him to go out of town, she does not know where he is; he does not call home. He will not buy any food or pay any utility bills. He will not go to church.

She said, "I work, and God supplies all my needs," but she wanted to know what to do. I had an answer for her. Boy, did I have an answer! But I thought I had better not give it. All I could do was tell her to pray. What do you tell somebody like that?

That is a classic example of a husband who is not carrying out the obligation of his marriage, nor is he providing for his own, nor is he walking in any of the responsibilities of a husband. I doubt if he is even saved.

LOVE MEANS TELLING THE TRUTH

Would Christ tell us the truth or lie to us? Then you ought to tell your wife the truth. Instead of looking at other women, tell your wife when she lets herself get out of shape. Have the decency and honesty to tell her. Then be an example yourself of what you expect from her. You cannot expect her to stay looking good if you are fat, sloppy, and out of shape. After all, when she married you, she did not marry the great white whale. It takes work and is a lifelong job, but it is worth it for your health as well as for your marriage.

Some of you do not like the way your wife dresses. Go and buy her the kind of clothes you do like. I want my wife to look the best, and I know what looks best on her better than anybody else.

Take the time and go shopping with her even if your feet do hurt. You find some sales people who will tell you the truth, but most of them will say anything to make a sale. Go with your wife and tell her what looks good. Sure it costs time. But it will cost you more if you do not go with her, because she has spent your money, and you may not like the dress. Ninety-nine percent of the time, I go with Betty to choose her clothes. I know what looks best on her. I want her to look good.

Of course, you need to use good sense. Don't go out and get yourself in debt buying clothes.

⋙✕⋘

LOVE MEANS CHERISHING YOUR WIFE

Paul said no man ever hates his own body but cherishes it even as the Lord the church (Eph. 5:29, KJV). That is how God treats us. He cherishes the Church. He takes care of us. He is always looking out for our welfare. He is always seeking for us to have the best.

Jesus said, "I came that you might have life," and that would have been enough, but He added *more,* and as if that were not enough, he added a superlative – *abundantly.* (John 10:10.) Life more abundantly is what He came for us to have. He cherished us.

So, husbands, we should cherish our wives. You have no right to wait until she acts right in order for you to treat her right. Your responsibility is to treat her right, no matter what she is doing. That is what the Word tells you to do. If she gets ugly, she must give account of that. You must give account if you do not treat her right. Your cherishing her should not be based on her doing all the things you want her to do. Nor should it be based on her agreeing with all of your idiosyncrasies. Your cherishing her and nourishing her should be based on the fact that the Word tells you to.

That is what Jesus does. Think about it. What if He treated us the way we treat Him? Thank God, He does not treat us in kind. He cherishes us out of a heart of love and puts up with all our mess. Because of that, we should be able to put up with one another.

LOVE HAS NO ROOM FOR BITTERNESS

Paul tells us in Colossians 3:19 (KJV):

Husbands, love your wives, and be not bitter against them.

A lot of men hold grudges against their wives for something they did years ago. They are bitter about it. Or a husband could be bitter at his wife for something his first wife, or some other woman in his life did. Because she was a woman, he has that attitude toward all women. If that is your case, then you need to forgive the one involved and turn loose of that bitterness. Suppose God held things against you? If anyone should be bitter about anything we do, it should be God.

If anyone has a right to be bitter, it is Jesus. After all, He is the One Who died for you, and you have just kicked up your heels and acted like a donkey with long ears. You acted ugly with God, and He just kept right on blessing you because you are in His family, and you are His child. He did not pull the carpet out from under you and leave you destitute.

How many times have you told the Lord, "Just let me get out of this, and I will serve You the balance of my days?"

Then when you got out of it, you forgot all about God. You might have meant it at the time, but you forgot, and it became a lie. So if anyone has a right to be bitter and hold something against us, it is God. So how dare we, as husbands, hold something against our wives?

You will have a right to hold something against her when you reach perfection. You can throw the first stone when you are without sin. But if you have not arrived at perfection yet, you had better forgive her as Christ has forgiven you.

Bitterness is not worth it, at any rate. Bitterness is from the devil. It will kill you. It will sour the sweetness in your spirit man. Bitterness does not come from the Spirit of God. I do not care what anyone has done to you or against you. It is not worth what bitterness will cost you.

CLEAVE *ONLY* TO YOUR WIFE

Genesis 2:24 (KJV) says a man shall leave his parents and **shall cleave unto his wife: and they shall be one flesh.**

God did not say that husband and wife were to be one with mother, father, sisters, cousins, brothers, aunts, Grandma and Grandpa, and the parakeet! When your wife married you, she did not marry your family.

Generally, it is w-r-o-n-g, wrong to have relatives living with you. Certainly it is wrong to take their side against your wife.

Your first obligation is to your wife. Your second is to your children by the wife you are presently married to. Your energies, your money, everything else belongs to the woman you marry.

Some men may weigh two hundred and sixty pounds and be six-feet-two and still be "Mama's little boy." I have heard of situations where the husband just suddenly told his wife, "Mama is coming to live with us."

That lady married you, Bud. She did not marry your mother, and you have no right to bring home any relatives against your wife's will. If you wanted to take care of your mother, you should have gotten a house and moved into it with her and never married.

The Bible did not say, "A man shall bring his mother and his father into his marriage with him."

God said to *leave* them. Do you know what *leave* means? He said you and the lady you marry are to be one flesh, not you and her parents and your parents. Your mother had her chance at bat. If she struck out, that is tough. I am sorry, but there is nothing I can do about it. You are not supposed to destroy or jeopardize your own family because your mother or father struck out in their own lives. They had their time at bat. That may sound hard, but it is the truth. Anything else is unfair.

Now let's talk about the exception to this truth. The exception is that you have a responsibility to do anything to help relatives that you can do *with your wife's agreement*. Your first duty is to her. If she does not go along with helping your family, then you have a challenge. You will need to do some praying! But you cannot give them money or bring them into the house without your wife's consent and be doing right.

Just because you are the head of the house, you have no right to take money from your wife and children to give to members of your family. Unless it is your *own* money. For example, if you and your wife have budgeted an allowance each, then in agreement, one or the other of you could use that money to give family members in need. But you should not take your paycheck and go pay your mama's rent, if your wife disagrees. That really amounts to stealing from your family.

Hopefully, if you and your wife both are saved, filled with the Spirit, and walking in the Word, you could sit down and come up with a plan to help them without hurting your own family. Usually, it is better not to move them into your own house – unless you have some unusual relatives, people who can live in your house and not interfere.

I know of one case where a man was living with his mother and taking care of her when he got married. He took his bride-to-be over to meet Mama, and everything was fine. Mama was real sweet and real nice until after that little girl became a part of the family. Then Mama started letting her hair down! Mama seemed like such a darling, then afterwards, she wanted to run the house.

If the husband loved his wife and wanted his marriage to work, he would have been foolish to answer his wife's complaints with, "Yeah, but you said it was all right for Mama to come and live with us."

Mama was tearing up his relationship. Things had changed. And Mama had to go. He had to lose a good wife or keep a no-good mother. Just because someone is a mother does not make them a nice person or of good character. We have institutionalized the word *mother* until it seems like *God*. We think mothers automatically are angels, when some mothers are devils.

Just to clear the air, let me tell you how my wife and I handled this situation in both our families.

❯❯❯❯❯ ✕ ❮❮❮❮❮

AGREE ON EXCEPTIONS TO THE RULE

Betty's mother was afflicted with a very severe case of arthritis more than twenty years ago. We attempted to help her spiritually, because we knew what God could do. For some reason, however, we never were able to get her to a point where she could receive healing. So she suffered. My wife felt an obligation to spend certain days of the week with her mother and help out in the home.

I could have been selfish and said, "No, you can't go over there. I married *you*. Your mother has her husband and other relatives. You stay home and take care of me."

But I did not do that. I knew how much it meant to her, so we *agreed* that she should help on a limited basis. Then we went one step farther as time went on. Betty and some of her brothers and sisters went together and paid for someone to come in and do the house cleaning.

I said, "All right. That is fine. That's the least we can do." We stayed in agreement over this.

Then a little later, one of the other relatives quit a job and moved into the house full time. Betty and the others went together and supported that person, so they all knew their parents had someone looking after them who really cared.

Then another situation arose on my side. My mother had been alone for a long time, because my father had died years ago. For various reasons, the house they lived in meant a lot to my mother. So she was going to hold on to that house, I figured, until the day she died. It was her security.

But when she was seventy-five years old, we began to discuss her situation. It was a shame for her to live by herself. One of our daughters had married, and we had an extra room. So Betty and I talked it over and decided to ask Mama to move in with us, to let her last days be her best days. Then she would not have to be concerned about living alone. She was still trying to earn a little extra money to help herself out. I felt she had already "paid her dues" in life – but I did not think she would move.

But when I asked her, she surprised me. Really, I was shocked! She was ready to leave. Now I did not just bring her in and say, "Mama is coming to live with us." My wife and I talked about it, worked things out, and got in agreement on it.

We told my mother she could sell her house and buy a new car, bank the rest of it, and live happily ever after. She would never have to buy any more groceries, pay another utility bill, or pay property taxes. She would have no responsibilities in the house, because I already have someone helping out.

She comes and goes as she pleases and does not have to lift a finger. It has turned out very well, because my mother is the kind of person who you do not even know is in the house. She does not try to tell us how to run our home, our marriage, or our family. It has been a beautiful situation.

But the only reason we had no trouble over the situation with her family or with my mother is that we communicated our thoughts and plans, and *we got in agreement with each other.*

If your wife is not in agreement, then you need to figure out what else can be done. Once you marry her, you become one flesh, and she has to come first.

Living by what our "guidebook," the Bible, says will result in the greatest degree of blessing, the greatest degree of love, and the greatest degree of fulfillment.

YOUR RELATIONSHIP WITH YOUR SPOUSE SCRIPTURES

Marriage should be honored by all, and the marriage bed kept pure, for God will judge the adulterer and all the sexually immoral.

Hebrews 13:4

A wife of noble character is her husband's crown, but a disgraceful wife is like decay in his bones.

Proverbs 12:4

Her children arise and call her blessed; her husband also, and he praises her. Her husband has full confidence in her and lacks nothing of value.

Proverbs 31:28,11

For example, by law a married woman is bound to her husband as long as he is alive, but if her husband dies, she is released from the law of marriage.

So then, if she marries another man while her husband is still alive, she is called an adulteress. But if her husband dies, she is released from that law and is not an adulteress, even though she marries another man.

Romans 7:2,3

But since there is so much immorality, each man should have his own wife, and each woman her own husband.

The husband should fulfill his marital duty to his wife, and likewise the wife to her husband.

The wife's body does not belong to her alone but also to her husband. In the same way, the husband's body does not belong to him alone but also to his wife.

To the married I give this command (not I, but the Lord): A wife must not separate from her husband.

But if she does, she must remain unmarried or else be reconciled to her husband. And a husband must not divorce his wife.

And if a woman has a husband who is not a believer and he is willing to live with her, she must not divorce him.

For the unbelieving husband has been sanctified through his wife, and the unbelieving wife has been sanctified through her believing husband. Otherwise your children would be unclean, but as it is, they are holy.

A woman is bound to her husband as long as he lives. But if her husband dies, she is free to marry anyone she wishes, but he must belong to the Lord.

1 Corinthians 7:2-4,10,11,13,14,39

However, each one of you also must love his wife as he loves himself, and the wife must respect her husband.

Ephesians 5:33

Wives, submit to your husbands as to the Lord.

For the husband is the head of the wife as Christ is the head of the church, his body, of which he is the Savior.

Now as the church submits to Christ, so also wives should submit to their husbands in everything.

Husbands, love your wives, just as Christ loved the church and gave himself up for her.

Ephesians 5:22-25

Wives, submit to your husbands, as is fitting in the Lord.
Husbands, love your wives and do not be harsh with them.

Colossians 3:18,19

Then they can train the younger women to love their husbands and children,

To be self-controlled and pure, to be busy at home, to be kind, and to be subject to their husbands, so that no one will malign the word of God.

Titus 2:4,5

Wives, in the same way be submissive to your husbands so that, if any of them do not believe the word, they may be won over without words by the behavior of their wives.

For this is the way the holy women of the past who put their hope in God used to make themselves beautiful. They were submissive to their own husbands.

Husbands, in the same way be considerate as you live with your wives, and treat them with respect as the weaker partner and as heirs with you of the gracious gift of life, so that nothing will hinder your prayers.

1 Peter 3:1,5,7

Your wife will be like a fruitful vine within your house; your sons will be like olive shoots around your table.

Psalm 128:3

May your fountain be blessed, and may you rejoice in the wife of your youth.

Proverbs 5:18

Houses and wealth are inherited from parents, but a prudent wife is from the Lord.

Proverbs 19:14

"Work began in the Garden of Eden. Adam was to dress the Garden and keep it. This work was an activity blessed of the Lord to provide Adam with a sense of achievement and self-worth. Take time to plan your career and life's work. It deserves your attention. Do not accept a job based simply on convenient location, or financial sufficiency or even friendship. Find what you are good at and do it with all your heart."

Mike Murdock

HONORING GOD IN YOUR WORK

"HONORING GOD ON YOUR JOB"

BY KENNETH COPELAND

Be Honorable, Not Slothful

Be kindly affectioned one to another with brotherly love; in honour preferring one another;
Not slothful in business....

Romans 12:10,11, KJV

The Apostle Paul tells us not to be lazy. There should not be an unwilling attitude where business is concerned between Christians. We should not be lazy and dishonorable in our dealings with anybody, especially not with our brothers and sisters in Christ.

This almost happened to me. I'm embarrassed to think how closely I came to doing the very thing I am warning you about.

I remember the day a young fellow came into my office and said he wanted to see me. I knew his folks so I let him in. He was excited.

"Brother Copeland," he said, "I've been listening to your tapes, and I've quit my job. I'm living by faith. I'm going in the ministry full time."

I thought, "Lord, he's going to be back through here before long begging for money."

The Lord said, "Well, when he does, give him some."

"What did You say?" I answered.

"When he does, give him some," repeated the Lord. "Don't ever sit in judgment against another person's faith. You had better pray and believe God for yourself. If you don't think he has the faith to carry this, get in with him and add your faith to his."

The message I received was: *Don't damn another person's faith.*

The young fellow I talked with that day was Jerry Savelle.

I didn't know what I was talking about. But by acting in honor (along with following some pointed guidance from the Lord) I was blessed to have a part in his eventual success and mighty ministry.

The minute Jerry walked out of the room, I realized that God was commissioning me to help teach and train that young man.

I would have missed that whole blessing if I had followed my own instincts and tried to talk him out of what he believed he was called to do.

I came close to being slothful in business (that is, in my business of being sensitive to God and helping spread His Word, directly or indirectly). God directed me to be fervent in spirit, to doubt not when dealing with a Christian brother or when serving the Lord.

BE FERVENT IN SPIRIT

...fervent in spirit; serving the Lord;

Rejoicing in hope; patient in tribulation; continuing instant in prayer;

Distributing to the necessity of saints; given to hospitality.

Bless them which persecute you: bless, and curse not.

Romans 12:11-14, KJV

Never lag in zeal or in earnest endeavor. Be aglow and burning with the Spirit, always eagerly and faithfully serving the Lord.

Don't go around with the corners of your mouth hanging down. Put on Jesus. Be like Jesus. Do as He would do.

Receive and exalt in hope, says the Apostle Paul. Be steadfast and patient in suffering and tribulation. Be constant in prayer.

In this passage Paul is describing the way we are to act in the Body of Christ. We are to keep our mouths shut about our own trials and tribulations, about our own hurts. We are not to go around rehearsing our problems all the time, repeating them to every preacher, minister and counselor we run across – again and again.

One of the reasons that we ministers of the gospel sometimes have to avoid our fellow Christians at meetings is because we cannot stay under the anointing if we constantly and repeatedly are being burdened with other people's trials and tribulations. Many people who do this don't really want help. They just want to go over their problem again and again and again, drawing attention to themselves. That's dishonorable.

God has said that our hurts are very important to Him. (1 Pet. 5:7.) However, they ought to mean little or nothing to us. We should be paying very little attention to our own problems and difficulties other than to take our stand of faith on God's Word and roll our cares over on Him and leave them there. He wants us to be alive with hope, not going around saying that things are hopeless all the time.

Be alive with hope. Be steadfast and patient in suffering. Don't worry about what is coming against you. Be strong in faith. Belittle your problems in the presence of others.

Quit carrying your burdens and cares around everywhere you go. Distribute to the needs of God's people. Share in meeting the necessities of the saints. Pursue the practice of hospitality. Bless those who persecute you, those who are cruel in their attitude toward you. Bless, and do not curse.

BE ABOUT THE BUSINESS

...I must be about my Father's business.

Luke 2:49, KJV

God does not want us to be slothful in conducting our business. He has honored us by seeing that we have it. We have to honor our obligation to Him by running that business or doing that job to the best of our abilities to do it in faith.

I'll give you an example. God has given me this ministry. He has given me the calling to minister. I have to honor that call and duty. I made a decision that I am going to live responsibly and honorably. I know Jesus wants me to do that, so I am determined to do it.

I promised God that any time I was called on to preach or minister, I would be ready; I would be prepared. That does not mean I want to all the time. It does not mean I am constantly, consistently prayed up and ready to go just on a second's notice. Most of the time I know in advance when I am going to preach.

I promised the Lord that I would never take time for myself and my own wants during the periods I should be preparing to minister to other people.

I am responsible for a prophetic ministry. When I travel from place to place on behalf of the Lord, I don't sightsee. I have been all over the world and have hardly seen anything but airports, hotels and convention centers. I don't go for pleasure or relaxation. I don't go to visit or fellowship. I go to do business. I take seriously Jesus' instructions to His disciples as He sent them out to minister. He said, "When you find a worthy house, stay there." (Matt. 10:11.) I don't run all over town. I come prepared, ready to settle down and attend to business – my Father's business.

I learned this originally from Oral Roberts; then I found it in the Word of God. Later, I saw it in Kenneth E. Hagin and in other anointed men of God.

I have certain time limits that I just won't violate. I may be in your presence sometime, look at my watch and say, "Excuse me, it's time to go." I do that because I am determined to have God's anointing on me. It is only with the anointing that I can, in turn, be of help to you at all. It is only through the anointing that I can minister effectively to others.

That is the reason all of my children are in the ministry. That is the reason there is romance in our family: between Gloria and me, our children and their mates and our grandchildren. My family and I honor the business – the ministry – that God has given us. We honor our obligations in a business-like manner. We honor one another, uplifting one another at all times. As a result we enjoy the blessing of God upon us.

❖

HONOR IS IMPORTANT IN BUSINESS

There is a man I want to tell you about. His story will help you see just how important it is to have honor in business – important in ways you may not have imagined.

This fellow was about 20 years old and had a good job. He came from a family that had very little money. He was the youngest child, and there was a lot of difficulty in his household. He worked his regular job all day, and at night fixed cars to sell. Gradually, he began making money.

He finally saved enough so he could buy a better type of car to restore and sell. He began to make a bit more money. He was good at his work, a gifted businessman.

His folks attended a Baptist church in Fort Worth. There was a meeting at church, and he decided to go. At the end of the service when the invitation was given, the conviction of the Holy Ghost came on him as he stood there. He had a tight grip on the seat in front of him, trying to resist responding to the wooing of the Lord.

The Spirit of God was all over him, and he was trying to keep from going forward and receiving Jesus as his Savior and Lord. A man in the church came over, put his arm around the young man and told him he loved him. He encouraged him to go forward. In fact, that man walked with him down the aisle.

Before that week was up, the same man who had led him to the altar to accept Jesus beat him out of all of his profit on a car. It wasn't a mistake. He just skinned that young man in a deal – on purpose. The older man should have known better. Any Christian ought to know that you don't get a man saved on Saturday night, then cheat him on Tuesday. That's wrong.

The young man had a temper. He was angry, so he rebelled against the Lord. He said he never would go back to church again. And he didn't.

He became very successful in the car business, and eventually had a business that was nationwide. Then he went into the airplane business, and I started flying for him. He and I became close friends.

My mother and father lived just two doors down from him. He liked my parents and would sometimes eat with us. Mama would feed him and preach to him and just love him. She would say, "I'm telling you right now, I'm going to pray you into the Kingdom of God." He would just smile.

She prayed for him just as she prayed for me – all the time. She treated him as if he were her own son, and he just ate it up. But she could not get him inside the church door. Why? Because of a dishonorable Christian businessman.

Years later, after I had entered the ministry I had the opportunity to pray with him. He stayed with it for a few days, then went right back to the way he had been. Afterwards, he stayed on my mind and heart a lot. I was praying about his situation once while I was in a meeting and I thought to myself, "I'm going to call him as soon as I get back to town."

When I got home and called him, a lady answered. When I asked if I could speak to him, she said, "He died day before yesterday."

You can imagine how I felt. I thought, "I missed him." Although I rolled the grief and pain over on the Lord, something in my spirit would not let it end that way.

I went to the funeral, and the man's son asked me to say a few words about his father. So I did. I told the people exactly what had happened in this man's life, what had caused him to be the way he was.

After the funeral when we were gathered at the memorial park, a woman walked up to me and said, "Kenneth, I need to tell you something." I want you to see God's faithfulness and honor from what she said.

GOD'S HONOR CAME THROUGH

I didn't know this woman. I had seen her, but was not acquainted with her personally.

"A few nights ago I absolutely could not sleep," she told me. "I tossed and turned, and finally got up to pray. 'God, what is this?' I asked.

"'Get dressed,' He answered. 'I've got somewhere I want you to go.'

"It was the middle of the night. I usually don't do things like that, but I obeyed the Lord. I got dressed, and then I asked, 'Where am I supposed to go?'

"He led me to a hospital, so I went.

"'I don't know anybody in this hospital,' I said. 'What do I do now, Lord?'

"He didn't say anything, so I just started praying in the Spirit as I walked down each hall. I don't know how many corridors I walked down, but it was several. I went along quietly just praying in the Spirit, listening for the Lord. Suddenly I stopped right in front of one room. The Lord said, 'Go in there.'

"I went in and saw that the man in the bed wasn't asleep. I walked up to him and said, 'Sir, I don't know you, and you don't know me. But the Lord wouldn't let me sleep tonight. God sent me down here to you. Do you know Jesus as Lord?'

"He said, 'You sound like Vinita and Kenneth Copeland.'

"'Vinita Copeland is a close personal friend of mine,' I told him.

"'I've been trying to call Kenneth for two days,' he answered. 'He's out of town, and I was lying here praying, "God, give me somebody. I'm dying. Send me somebody. I can't die in this shape. I can't die like this. Send me somebody, Lord. Send me somebody."'"

What was happening in that situation? God's honor was at work. God was honoring the decision that man made back in the Baptist church nearly 40 years before. He was honoring my mother's prayers and my prayers and our love for that man. God was honoring all these things.

Thank God for that woman who honored God's direction to go to that hospital in the middle of the night, not even knowing why. She prayed with him, and he came back to Jesus, praying and rejoicing in Him.

Then he died.

Actually, he didn't die. He just stepped out of that old cancerous body in which he was confined and went on to be with the Lord.

This man finally recognized the honor of God in the last minute of the last hour. Thank God for that! Think what just one act by a dishonorable Christian had done. Because of that one shameful dealing, another man had spent his entire life out of fellowship with Jesus, his brothers and sisters in the Lord, and with the Father Himself.

YOUR WORK SCRIPTURES

Your Relationship With Your Employer

Slaves, obey your earthly masters with respect and fear, and with sincerity of heart, just as you would obey Christ.

Obey them not only to win their favor when their eye is on you, but like slaves of Christ, doing the will of God from your heart.

Serve wholeheartedly, as if you were serving the Lord, not men,

Because you know that the Lord will reward everyone for whatever good he does, whether he is slave or free.

Ephesians 6:5-8

Slaves, obey your earthly masters in everything; and do it, not only when their eye is on you and to win their favor, but with sincerity of heart and reverence for the Lord.

Whatever you do, work at it with all your heart, as working for the Lord, not for men,

Since you know that you will receive an inheritance from the Lord as a reward. It is the Lord Christ you are serving.

Colossians 3:22-24

All who are under the yoke of slavery should consider their masters worthy of full respect, so that God's name and our teaching may not be slandered.

Those who have believing masters are not to show less respect for them because they are brothers. Instead, they are to serve them even better, because those who benefit from their service are believers, and dear to them. These are the things you are to teach and urge on them.

1 Timothy 6:1,2

Teach slaves to be subject to their masters in everything, to try to please them, not to talk back to them.

Titus 2:9

Slaves, submit yourselves to your masters with all respect, not only to those who are good and considerate, but also to those who are harsh.

1 Peter 2:18

He who tends a fig tree will eat its fruit, and he who looks after his master will be honored.

Proverbs 27:18

Who then is the faithful and wise servant, whom the master has put in charge of the servants in his household to give them their food at the proper time?

It will be good for that servant whose master finds him doing so when he returns.

I tell you the truth, he will put him in charge of all his possessions.

But suppose that servant is wicked and says to himself, "My master is staying away a long time,"

And he then begins to beat his fellow servants and to eat and drink with drunkards.

The master of that servant will come on a day when he does not expect him and at an hour he is not aware of.

He will cut him to pieces and assign him a place with the hypocrites, where there will be weeping and gnashing of teeth.

Matthew 24:45-51

It will be good for those servants whose master finds them watching when he comes. I tell you the truth, he will dress himself to serve, will have them recline at the table and will come and wait on them.

Luke 12:37

Whoever can be trusted with very little can also be trusted with much, and whoever is dishonest with very little will also be dishonest with much.

Luke 16:10

And if you have not been trustworthy with someone else's property, who will give you property of your own?

Luke 16:12

I tell you the truth, no servant is greater than his master, nor is a messenger greater than the one who sent him.

John 13:16

Now it is required that those who have been given a trust must prove faithful.

1 Corinthians 4:2

YOUR RELATIONSHIP WITH YOUR EMPLOYEES

Do not defraud your neighbor or rob him. Do not hold back the wages of a hired man overnight.

Leviticus 19:13

Do not take advantage of a hired man who is poor and needy, whether he is a brother Israelite or an alien living in one of your towns.

Pay him his wages each day before sunset, because he is poor and is counting on it. Otherwise he may cry to the Lord against you, and you will be guilty of sin.

Deuteronomy 24:14,15

Woe to him who builds his palace by unrighteousness, his upper rooms by injustice, making his countrymen work for nothing, not paying them for their labor.

Jeremiah 22:13

Take no bag for the journey, or extra tunic, or sandals or a staff; for the worker is worth his keep.

Matthew 10:10

Those who have believing masters are not to show less respect for them because they are brothers. Instead, they are to serve them even better, because those who benefit from their service are believers, and dear to them. These are the things you are to teach and urge on them.

1 Timothy 6:2

Now when a man works, his wages are not credited to him as a gift, but as an obligation.

Romans 4:4

And masters, treat your slaves in the same way. Do not threaten them, since you know that he who is both their Master and yours is in heaven, and there is no favoritism with him.

Ephesians 6:9

Masters, provide your slaves with what is right and fair, because you know that you also have a Master in heaven.

Colossians 4:1

For the Scripture says, "Do not muzzle the ox while it is treading out the grain," and "The worker deserves his wages."

1 Timothy 5:18

"Wake up to the abundance of heaven that's been made yours through Jesus. Wake up to the fact that you've been translated out of a world of poverty into a kingdom of abundance. Rejoice. Heaven's unlimited resources have been made available to you!"

Kenneth Copeland

FINANCIAL MANAGEMENT

"GOD WANTS YOU TO PROSPER"

BY JOHN AVANZINI

Third John 2 (KJV) says:

> Beloved, I wish *above all things* that thou mayest prosper and be in *health,* even as thy soul *prospereth.*

Did you hear that fantastic news? God wants you to prosper.

Notice the *high priority* He gives to your prospering. God wants it for you *above all things*! Above all things in the universe, God wants you to prosper. Above all things in the galaxy, God wants you to prosper. Even as God sustains all the molecules and matter in His magnificent creation, He has as *His primary desire, that you prosper.*

His prosperity is total. God wants to prosper you *mentally*; He wants you to be at peace.

> Peace I leave you, my peace I give unto you: not as the world giveth, give I unto you.
>
> John 14:27, KJV

Notice your peace is already here, and in great abundance. Jesus said: *My peace I leave you.* Your peace is not way off somewhere in a distant land called heaven. It is right here and now! It is not in the future; grasp that. He said: **My peace I give unto you....**

The present tense. Your peace, your mental prosperity, is provided by your loving God *in the now.*

God also wants you to prosper physically – to be in good health, to have health in great abundance, He took on Himself cruel stripes that purchased health for all.

In Isaiah 53:5 (KJV) we read: **...and with his stripes we are healed.** The present tense.

There is more than enough health for you, and it is provided by your loving God *in the now*.

God also wants you to prosper (present tense) in your finances. Look at Second Peter 1:3 (KJV):

According as his divine power hath given unto us all things (total, complete) **that pertain unto life....**

God desires that you prosper *financially*. He has already provided for your financial prosperity *in the now*.

All of this prosperity – mental, physical, and financial – *is yours now! But*, notice a critical condition: *Even as your soul prospers*.

God tells us to take care of the inner man, to be right with Him in all things.

Feed your inner man. Keep him on a good, healthy diet of God's Word. Place him on a good exercise program of doing God's will. Enroll him in a good mental hygiene program, thinking only about the good things of God. *Then*, as your soul prospers, *so, too*, will your health and finances.

Don't you just feel in your heart that as you draw nearer to the Lord, He will draw nearer to you? The Word says it is so in James 4:8.

Don't you just know that as you put this great body of truth about giving and receiving from God to work for you, your prosperity in the financial realm is already becoming a reality?

For those who flow in His will, the Bible clearly states it is *His desire* that you prosper. The two points are connected; your earthly prosperity as God's child is tied directly to your spiritual prosperity.

But thou shalt remember the Lord thy God: for it is he that *giveth* **thee power to get wealth, that he may establish his covenant which he sware unto thy fathers, as it is this day.**

Deuteronomy 8:18, KJV

God not only wants you to prosper, but He gives you the power to get wealth. For so long, I thought it was godly to be poor. For so long, I thought going without things was an act of contrition on my part, and somehow believed my dedication to poverty impressed God. But that is not what the Bible says.

He wants you to prosper, and He gives you the power to get wealth. God has a covenant with you. If you understand God and His Word, and if your life is one that abides in His will, then the Lord has a covenant of blessing for your life.

"But Brother John, you know, money is the root of all evil," Mr. Skeptic smugly shouts. "The Bible teaches that, you know."

Skeptic, hold on to your skeptical halo. The Word of God *does not say* that money is the root of all evil. In First Timothy 6:10 (KJV), it reads:

For the love of money is the root of all evil, which while some coveted after, they have erred from the faith, and pierced themselves through with many sorrows.

The *love of money* is the root of all evil. If the money itself were evil, *God would not give you the power to obtain it*. He does promise that as His *obedient* child, you will receive plenty of wealth, as long as you do not develop a *love* for it.

This is the whole purpose for God's giving us wealth; He expects us to spread His Word. Wealth derived for the wrong purpose would never make you happy. If it did, then no one with money would ever commit suicide or go into divorce court or have a drinking problem. Wealth not received from God will not make you happy. Many times people with the most money are also those with the most misery.

When wealth is obtained through God's plan, it comes with the promise that it will make you happy – without sorrow. Proverbs 10:22 (KJV) states:

The blessing of the Lord, it maketh rich, and he addeth no sorrow with it.

What type of riches causes sorrow? The type we desperately try to hold on to, the riches that mean so much to us that their loss would be a major crisis in life.

God's wealth is different. It is a wealth *to be given away*!

Once again we see that God's wisdom is foolishness in the world. Givers get, to give again – to Him, for His glory.

If it were not for the greed of man, there would be more than enough abundance on earth. There is more than enough money on earth right now for every man, woman, boy and girl to live like a millionaire! That's right, all four and a half *billion* people on this earth could live like millionaires were it not for the greed of man!

As you start receiving from God as you apply His laws, do not let greed get in the way of His purpose. As you receive, turn right around and give a generous measure back into His ministries. Give the tithe; get those windows of heaven open in your life. Give great, generous offerings to those places God tells you to, so that a good measure will be poured out to you through the open windows of heaven.

Be careful that the abundance of your life does not start to make you greedy. Let God shine through all of your life, especially through your financial matters. The only wealth that will not bring sorrow is the wealth that you control, the wealth that does not control you, wealth *you do not love*, but are willing to put back into the Gospel of God.

Ecclesiastes 10:19 (KJV) says, **...money answereth all things.** Is your money doing that? Is your money building God's Kingdom or building your kingdom? Remember Luke 6:38 (KJV):

Give, and it shall be given unto you; good measure, pressed down, and shaken together, and running over, shall men give into your bosom. For with the same measure that ye mete (measure), **it shall be measured to you again.**

Remember, there is more than enough for the man or woman who is a gracious giver, and by putting the principles you have just read into practice, you, too, can soon be always abounding in the good things of God.

YOUR FINANCES SCRIPTURES

But as for you, be strong and do not give up, for your work will be rewarded.

2 Chronicles 15:7

Lazy hands make a man poor, but diligent hands bring wealth.

Proverbs 10:4

Diligent hands will rule, but laziness ends in slave labor.

Proverbs 12:24

The sluggard craves and gets nothing, but the desires of the diligent are fully satisfied.

Proverbs 13:4

Plans fail for lack of counsel, but with many advisers they succeed.

Proverbs 15:22

He who is kind to the poor lends to the Lord, and he will reward him for what he has done.

Proverbs 19:17

Do not love sleep or you will grow poor; stay awake and you will have food to spare.

Proverbs 20:13

Do you see a man skilled in his work? He will serve before kings; he will not serve before obscure men.

Proverbs 22:29

He who works his land will have abundant food, but the one who chases fantasies will have his fill of poverty.

Proverbs 28:19

But seek first his kingdom and his righteousness, and all these things will be given to you as well.

Matthew 6:33

Be sure you know the condition of your flocks, give careful attention to your herds.

Proverbs 27:23

And my God will meet all your needs according to his glorious riches in Christ Jesus.

Philippians 4:19

Dear friend, I pray that you may enjoy good health and that all may go well with you, even as your soul is getting along well.

3 John 2

Honor the Lord with your wealth, with the firstfruits of all your crops; then your barns will be filled to overflowing, and your vats will brim over with new wine.

Proverbs 3:9,10

He who gives to the poor will lack nothing, but he who closes his eyes to them receives many curses.

Proverbs 28:27

Cast your bread upon the waters, for after many days you will find it again.

Ecclesiastes 11:1

"Bring the whole tithe into the storehouse, that there may be food in my house. Test me in this," says the Lord Almighty, "and see if I will not throw open the floodgates of heaven and pour out so much blessing that you will not have room enough for it.

"I will prevent pests from devouring your crops, and the vines in your fields will not cast their fruit," says the Lord Almighty.

Malachi 3:10,11

Give, and it will be given to you. A good measure, pressed down, shaken together and running over, will be poured into your lap. For with the measure you use, it will be measured to you.

Luke 6:38

If anyone has material possessions and sees his brother in need but has no pity on him, how can the love of God be in him?

Dear children, let us not love with words or tongue but with actions and in truth.

1 John 3:17,18

"Many charismatics have insecure children. This is simply because they are putting everything else ahead of their children. You may win five hundred million people to God, but it will count exactly zero if you lose the three or four souls in your own home. According to the Word of God, your first responsibility is to your children."

Kenneth Hagin, Jr.

FAMILY ENRICHMENT

"THE MAKING OF A FAMILY"

BY RICHARD EXLEY

The family is not a cultural phenomenon to be discarded with the changing times. It was conceived in the mind of God. It is the loving gift of a wise and generous Creator. Knowing the unique needs of the man created in His own image, God said: **...It is not good for the man to be alone. I will make a helper suitable for him** (Gen. 2:18).

> **...So the Lord God caused the man to fall into a deep sleep; and while he was sleeping, he took one of the man's ribs and closed up the place with flesh. Then the Lord God made a woman from the rib he had taken out of the man, and he brought her to the man.**

> **Genesis 2:21,22**

Now the man is no longer alone. He has a companion, someone to love and someone to love him, and a helper. Think of that – God made them helpers, one for the other. And He blessed that union and called it "family." Therefore, we must conclude that God intended for the family to be a helping place. And when it functions as God intended, that's what it is. It provides a loving community in which a child is "helped" to develop his gifts and potentials. It is a safe place in which a child is "helped" to develop the people skills so necessary to live meaningfully in our complex society. And it is a sanctuary in which he is "helped" to learn spiritual values and develop a personal relationship with the living God.

Obviously the most important thing in creating a family is time – time to be together, time to love one another, time to share life's experiences, both great and small. Unfortunately, time seems to be the thing we find hardest to give.

In *What Wives Wish Their Husbands Knew About Women*, Dr. Dobson quotes from an article by Dr. Branfenbrenner, in which he decries the plague of parental absence: "The demands of a job that claim meal times, evenings and weekends as well as day; the trips and moves necessary to get ahead or simply to hold one's own; the increasing time spent communicating, entertaining, going out, meeting social and community obligations, all these produce a situation in which a child often spends more time with a passive babysitter than with a participating parent."[1]

Dr. Dobson then proceeds to substantiate Branfenbrenner's observations: "A team of researchers wanted to learn how much time middle-class fathers spend playing and interacting with their small children. First, they asked a group of fathers to estimate the time spent with their one-year-old youngsters each day, and received an average reply of fifteen to twenty minutes. To verify these claims, the investigators attached microphones to the shirts of small children for the purpose of recording actual parental verbalization. The results were shocking: *The average amount of time spent by these middle-class fathers with their small children was thirty-seven seconds per day!* Their direct interaction was limited to 2.7 encounters daily lasting ten to fifteen seconds each."[2] (Emphasis mine.)

It goes almost without saying that the children of such fathers will grow up lacking the sense of family which is absolutely vital to a healthy self-image. Depending upon their motivation, their skills, and their intellect, they may go on to become outstanding successes in their chosen fields. But without a special healing they will not be fulfilled; they will not escape the nagging questions they have about their value as persons. Still, the greatest tragedy may be the fact that they will "sin" against their children in the same way their parents "sinned" against them, thus perpetuating this tragedy from generation to generation. And the likelihood of this happening increases, almost daily, as our world becomes more and more impersonal.

In order to break this deadly cycle, the person driven by self-doubts must find emotional healing in the presence of God, and through the dynamic fellowship of committed believers. He must find a surrogate family, a place to belong. As unlikely as this may sound to the person who has been "alone" all his life, it is possible. In fact, it is happening with increasing frequency. As the Church learns more and more about the relationship between community and personal wholeness, it is providing greater ministry in this area. Over and over again, through the years, I have witnessed God's healing love manifested through small groups of loving believers. The miracles are seldom instantaneous, but they are, nonetheless, dramatic. Take the case of Sterling, for instance:

"I first met him when he came to my office for pastoral counseling. He was only a few days removed from the county jail and newly converted....

"He never knew his father, and his mother abandoned him when he was just a small boy. A kindly aunt took him in and reared him as her own. Still, her love could not heal the wound his parents' rejection had inflicted. By the time he was fourteen, he was a confirmed alcoholic and constantly in trouble with the authorities.

"His incorrigible behavior finally resulted in his being sent to reform school. Unfortunately, that intensified his anger and bitterness, and upon his release he immediately returned to his antisocial behavior. Soon he was serving a sentence in the state penitentiary, then another.

"When he came to see me, he was out on bail awaiting trial for allegedly raping his sixteen-year-old stepdaughter. While in the county jail, he had started reading the Bible and was born again. Now he wanted to know if he could become part of our church. I assured him that he could, and soon he was deeply involved in the life of our fellowship including a growth group which I led once a week. I can still remember the night he told us that he finally felt loved, for the first time in his life, by God and by the group."[3]

At last he was free from his parents' rejection and the debilitating wounds it had left. Now he could get on with the business of becoming a loving husband and father in his own right. It wouldn't be easy, because he had a lifetime of negative behavior to "unlearn," but he knew that with God's help and the support of the group it was possible.

I share Sterling's story, extreme though it is, to make a point. If God could do that for him, then surely He can heal the fears and insecurities that haunt you. There is hope for your family!

And, even if you grew up in a family rich with love and acceptance, you will still need God's help to be the kind of parent your children need. Given the pressures we all face, only a determined decision, backed up by divine help, will enable us to give our families the spiritual and emotional support they must have. As I look back over the past 22 years of marriage, I can testify to God's sufficiency and His faithfulness.

Until Leah entered the fifth grade, her mother and I were serving pastorates in small churches in remote rural areas. Financially, it was a hardship, but what we lacked in money was more than made up for in family time. My office was in the house, so I was always near Leah. Some of my best memories are of her interrupting my sermon preparation for a little tender loving care. Until she was in the sixth grade I was able to drive her to school every morning and pick her up every afternoon. Those were our special times. I'll never forget how she looked bounding down the hill toward the car, her fists full of papers, her hair backlighted by the afternoon sun.

Inspired by the example left us by our parents, Brenda and I determined to continue the holy heritage of family. In the winter we all went snowmobiling in the countryside and ice skating in the park. In the summer we hiked and picnicked in the mountains. In the fall we cut firewood, buoyed by the prospect of long winter evenings together in front of a roaring fire. We became "photography nuts," and we now have hundreds of pictures, and even more memories.

I will always be thankful I was free to be a father when Leah needed me most. Still, it was a choice. There were many things I could have done, but I chose to spend my time and energy being a husband and a father. What are you choosing?

In addition to time, children must have unconditional parental love if they are to grow up to be emotionally whole adults. In my work with professional groups, I frequently encounter men and women who overreact to the smallest slight, real or imagined. Others are defensive, while still others are withdrawn or have trouble relating to persons in authority. Again and again these difficulties have their roots in the parent-child relationship. As a general rule such people did not receive their parents' unconditional love when they were children. As a consequence, they are not emotionally whole persons.

Unconditional love is not dependent upon the child's performance. It is given freely, consistently. It enables a child to unconsciously separate his value as a person from his performance, good or bad. Unconditional love can be expressed in a variety of ways, but none is more effective than touching and telling. All children need to be held and hugged. They need to hear their parents say the three most powerful words in the human vocabulary – "I love you."

Almost four years ago, I was on my way to Anchorage, Alaska, and I finally had a few hours to myself. There were no phones to answer, no deadlines to meet, and no one scheduled for counseling. After a couple of hours I began to wind down, and as I did, I grew nostalgic, or philosophical, maybe both. Not being one to waste such feelings, I wrote my daughter a letter. I would like to share some of it with you:

"Dear Leah,

"It's been a while since I've told you what a special person you are. God has given you the gift of joy and self-confidence. I think you have tremendous people skills, and a real talent for public speaking and drama. When I was your age I was shy and introverted; my gifts were not developed at all. You are years ahead of me and I believe your accomplishments will far exceed my own. Never forget, though, that when God gives a person special gifts, He also gives them special responsibilities.

"I hope I've rubbed off on you these past fifteen years. I want you to catch the values which make my life rich. Here's a partial list of the things I hope you remember when you are grown and on your own.

"1. Attitude is everything – it can make or break you. It is the one thing no one can ever take from you – the freedom to choose how you are going to feel about a given situation. As the poet put it, 'Two men looked out through the prison bars; one man saw the mud, one man saw the stars.'

"2. Relationships are the most important things in life. Do unto others as you would have them do unto you. Always be careful to use things and love people.

"3. Don't be afraid to fail. Nothing great was ever achieved on the first try. Learn from your failures and try again.

"4. God's will is not inhibiting. It frees you to fulfill your highest potential, while enjoying the most meaningful life possible.

"5. If you sin, God always stands ready to forgive. In fact, He is always more anxious to forgive us than we are to be forgiven.

"6. True joy is found in striving for God-given goals, even more than in obtaining them; so dare to dream big dreams, dare to attempt great things for God.

"That's enough for today. Let me close with some things I hope you remember when you are grown and gone. I hope you remember how crazy funny I can be when it's just the three of us and I'm letting my hair down. I hope you remember how much I love your mother and how special I think she is. I hope you remember how conscientious I was, how hard I worked, and how deeply I cared for people. Most of all I want you to remember how much I love God and how special you are to me. Never forget that I love you unconditionally. There is nothing you can do, no success or achievement, which will ever make me love you more. I love you, not because of what you do, but because of who you are.

"With all my love,

"Dad"

Boys need that kind of affirming love, too. Betsy Lee, in *Miracle in the Making*, writes: "My mother grew up in a family of girls. She was comfortable raising my sister and me, but my brother John confounded her from the day he was born.

"Distance loomed between Mom and John. She wasn't sure how to express her affection or tame his wild spirit. She seemed constantly to warn him of dangers.

"John frequently whined, 'You're always telling me that.'

"Mother always explained that her instructions were for his benefit. 'What do you think a mother is for?' she added.

"'To love me,' he said.

"My mother was stunned, but prudent enough not to be defensive. She sought to change the way she communicated her love.

"My aunt, who had raised a son, told my mother, 'Boys aren't any different from girls. They need to be touched and kissed goodnight.' This came as a revelation to my mother, who thought cuddling would compromise her son's masculinity. But as soon as she started to demonstrate her love in direct, visible ways, John responded with greater warmth, and he began to respect her authority.

"As in all relationships, love had to be expressed in words and actions in order to grow."[4]

Some parents get the wrong impression when we talk of loving our children unconditionally. They mistakenly think that means they should never discipline their offspring. Nothing could be further from the truth. In fact, without proper discipline children will be unsure of their parents' love. When used appropriately, discipline is an act of love; it also creates a feeling of security by clearly defining the boundaries of behavior.

Discipline without love is tyrannical; it produces dependent people who are both hostile and fearful. Love without discipline is permissive; it trains children to be selfish and obnoxious. But when unconditional love and consistent discipline are both present in the family structure, they produce children who are emotionally healthy and well-adjusted.

"Dr. Stanley Coopersmith, associate professor of psychology, University of California, studied 1,738 normal middle-class boys and their families, beginning in the pre-adolescent period and following them through to young manhood. After identifying those boys having the highest self-esteem, he compared their homes and childhood influences with those having a lower sense of self-worth. He found three important characteristics which distinguished them:

"1. The high-esteem children clearly were more loved and appreciated at home than were the low-esteem boys.

"2. The high-esteem group came from homes where parents had been significantly more strict in their approach to discipline. By contrast, the parents of the low-esteem group had created insecurity and dependence by their permissiveness.

"3. The homes of the high-esteem group were also characterized by democracy and openness. Once the boundaries for behavior were established, there was freedom for individual personalities to grow and develop. The boys could express themselves without fear of ridicule, and the overall atmosphere was marked by acceptance and emotional safety."[5]

To fully satisfy the growing child's spiritual and emotional needs, the family must also provide spiritual training. While this should definitely include some form of graduated family devotions, designed with the child's needs in mind, in truth the most effective training grows out of real-life experiences. The most productive parents are those who watch for these special moments and make the most of them.

It has been called "striking while the iron is hot," a phrase which comes out of the old village blacksmith's shop. It refers to that precise moment when the metal has been heated to the exact temperature at which it is the most malleable. Life, too, has a way of creating situations like that in the experience of every child. Moments when circumstances have sensitized him to spiritual truths. The perceptive parent seizes those opportunities and, as a result, life-transforming truth is planted deep in the child's soul.

Take the time to allow your family to develop as God intended. Take the time to help your children develop their gifts and potentials, their people skills. Take the time to help them learn spiritual values and to form a deep personal relationship with the living God. And take the time to be together, to love one another, to share life's experiences both great and small.

---

[1] James Dobson. *What Wives Wish Their Husbands Knew About Women.* Wheaton: Tyndale House Publishers, Inc., 1975, p. 158.

[2] Ibid.

[3] Richard Exley. *Blue-Collar Christianity.* Tulsa: Honor Books, 1989, pp. 193,194.

[4] Reprinted by permission from *Miracle in the Making* by Betsy Lee, 1983, Augsburg Publishing House.

[5] James Dobson. *Hide and Seek, Self-Esteem for the Child.* Old Tappan: Fleming H. Revell, 1979, pp. 92,93.

YOUR RELATIONSHIP WITH
YOUR CHILDREN SCRIPTURES

He settles the barren woman in her home as a happy mother of children. Praise the Lord.

Psalm 113:9

Remember the day you stood before the Lord your God at Horeb, when he said to me, "Assemble the people before me to hear my words so that they may learn to revere me as long as they live in the land and may teach them to their children."

Deuteronomy 4:10

These commandments that I give you today are to be upon your hearts. Impress them on your children. Talk about them when you sit at home and when you walk along the road, when you lie down and when you get up.

Deuteronomy 6:6,7

Fix these words of mine in your hearts and minds; tie them as symbols on your hands and bind them on your foreheads.

Teach them to your children, talking about them when you sit at home and when you walk along the road, when you lie down and when you get up.

Deuteronomy 11:18,19

Jesus said, "Let the little children come to me, and do not hinder them, for the kingdom of heaven belongs to such as these."

Matthew 19:14

Whoever welcomes one of these little children in my name welcomes me; and whoever welcomes me does not welcome me but the one who sent me.

Mark 9:37

If you then, though you are evil, know how to give good gifts to your children, how much more will your Father in heaven give the Holy Spirit to those who ask him!

Luke 11:13

If you, then, though you are evil, know how to give good gifts to your children, how much more will your Father in heaven give good gifts to those who ask him!

Matthew 7:11

The promise is for you and your children and for all who are far off – for all whom the Lord our God will call.

Acts 2:39

For the unbelieving husband has been sanctified through his wife, and the unbelieving wife has been sanctified through her believing husband. Otherwise your children would be unclean, but as it is, they are holy.

1 Corinthians 7:14

Now I am ready to visit you for the third time, and I will not be a burden to you, because what I want is not your possessions but you. After all, children should not have to save up for their parents, but parents for their children.

2 Corinthians 12:14

Children, obey your parents in the Lord, for this is right.
"Honor your father and mother" – which is the first commandment with a promise –
"That it may go well with you and that you may enjoy long life on the earth."
Fathers, do not exasperate your children; instead, bring them up in the training and instruction of the Lord.

Ephesians 6:1-4

Children, obey your parents in everything, for this pleases the Lord.
Fathers, do not embitter your children, or they will become discouraged.

Colossians 3:20,21

For you know that we dealt with each of you as a father deals with his own children.

1 Thessalonians 2:11

He must manage his own family well and see that his children obey him with proper respect.

A deacon must be the husband of but one wife and must manage his children and his household well.

1 Timothy 3:4,12

An elder must be blameless, the husband of but one wife, a man whose children believe and are not open to the charge of being wild and disobedient.

Titus 1:6

Then they can train the younger women to love their husbands and children.

Titus 2:4

Discipline your son, for in that there is hope; do not be a willing party to his death.

Proverbs 19:18

Do not withhold discipline from a child; if you punish him with the rod, he will not die.

Punish him with the rod and save his soul from death.

Proverbs 23:13,14

The righteous man leads a blameless life; blessed are his children after him.

Proverbs 20:7

Train a child in the way he should go, and when he is old he will not turn from it.

Proverbs 22:6

"Anyone who believes they can enjoy sexual relations with more than one person and shake it off as some superficial part of their lives is into confusion. In the Garden of Eden, God established a spiritual bond between husband and wife which is the basis for all sexual morality and purity. When sexual fidelity is practiced, the marriage will bring peace and prosperity to the home."

Bob Yandian

SEXUAL FULFILLMENT

"GOD MADE SEX GOOD"

BY EDWIN LOUIS COLE

God made sex good!

As long as I live I shall never forget the day in a seminar at a Holiday Inn in Irving, Texas, when I made that statement and three hundred Texans all shouted, "Amen!"

All I could think of was three hundred wives calling me, wanting to know what under God's heaven I had said to their husbands.

Yet, the truth is that God made sex good, made it to be the most desirable thing for a man in relationship to a woman so the earth would be replenished, or repopulated, and thus fulfill God's command. God made sex good so that man would not feel forced to replenish the earth. He also made it good for man's pleasure because He loved the man.

Sex is not something to be ashamed of, avoided, denied or secretly lusted after. It is something lovely, good, holy, decent and in keeping with the covenant relationship between a man and wife.

In creation, God created the entire earth in the positive.

Man through sin recreated it in the negative.

Sin always promises to serve and please, but only desires to enslave and dominate. That's true of alcohol, drugs, pornography, greed, jealousy, and every other sin of the flesh and spirit.

God creates, Satan counterfeits.

The corner barroom is a counterfeit church. The bartender is the pastor, people go in to find fellowship, get counsel, and are filled with the spirit(s).

There is a freedom that comes from love, but lust gives a heavy burden. *Love is satisfying, lust is insatiable.*

Just as hell is never satisfied, neither is the lust of the flesh. Lust is degenerative. From fantasies, sexual lust descends in its unbridled thirst to sado-masochism, then to bestiality, and finally to murder itself. Over 50,000 murders per year occur in America through sexual deviation.

The latest serial murderer I've read about was arrested for thirty-seven murders, all of them committed because of sexual deviation and perversion of the accused.

There is no joy in lust. Lust is a counterfeit of love.

Prayer produces intimacy, but pornography is a substitute for prayer. Pornography promises to serve and please, but only enslaves and dominates. One psychologist stated that it takes four to five years of therapy to rid patients of sexual addictions. God can do it better.

The mores of society are imposing themselves on the Church, instead of the Church establishing the mores of society. Rather than be embarrassed by, criticize, or find fault with the men who are openly contending for righteousness in our society, we need to thank God for them, pray for them, and stand with them.

Pornography has made oral sex popular with the lustful, and a problem for the loving. A pastor asked me to speak at a women's luncheon, and then gave the ladies slips of paper on which to write their questions for me to answer. Eight out of ten questions were, "What do you say about oral sex?"

A woman called our office asking for help because her husband had put her out of the house when she refused to engage in oral sex. She wanted to know what the Bible said about it.

The fact is, the Bible says nothing about it directly.

However, the Bible says plenty about love and sex.

Just as God did not force man to procreate, but instead made sex an enjoyable act that man would desire, so the man must treat his wife – not forcing anything on her but making the sex act enjoyable so she will desire it. The sexual union is directly related to a man's loving his wife even as Christ also loved the Church. Any man who *forces* his wife to engage in sexual acts *of any kind* is operating out of lust, not love.

One man wrote that he and his wife didn't have any problems, except one – she didn't want to have oral sex. The disagreement about oral sex was not "his only problem," it was an indication and outgrowth of more serious underlying problems. Dealing with surface issues will never clear up deep-seated hurts, attitudes and beliefs.

If people were more educated concerning God's view of sex, the sacredness of the covenant, and if they had more fear of the Lord in their lives, there would not be a need to address these concerns.

Whatsoever is not of faith is sin, is what Romans 14:23 (KJV) says.

Any time a man forces his wife to do something contrary to her consecration, and coerces her to do something outside of faith, it is sin. There is generally a basic attitude of lust versus love in the argument.

But here is a letter which reveals what happens when a man meets God.

"I praise God for the mighty work He has done and is doing through you, Brother Cole! My husband Rick attended the seminar you held in Chicago, and I had to write and tell you what the Lord has done.

"We had been married for about ten years. The first couple of years we were too dumb to know we had problems, and during the next four years our marriage relationship deteriorated until our family life had become almost unbearable. I thought I knew the Lord, but I finally was scared enough to get serious about straightening out my relationship with the Lord Jesus. And I began to pray, only with a 'can't-You-do-anything-about-this-jerk-I'm-living-with' attitude.

"Well, one night while I was reading the Bible, I read Ephesians 5:22-24. Something (Someone, really) deep inside me said, 'This is for you.' I thought, 'Oh, no it's not,' and tried to keep right on reading. 'Far be it from me to submit to a man who's into drugs and alcohol, and doesn't even know You, Lord!' I thought. But that 'something' deep inside said gently, 'If you won't, you're a hypocrite.'

"I wrestled with that for weeks. Every scripture I read convicted me on the subject – everything in the circumstances seemed to prove that it would be the most foolish decision possible. My daughter was still breast-feeding, we had no money, Rick was leaving us 'for good' about twice a month, and was angry because I wouldn't smoke dope with him and his friends. But the conviction continued. My heart still reads Matthew 5:47 like this, 'And if you submit to Christ-like husbands only, what do you more than others?'

"Finally, I did submit to God *and* my husband, and got busy seeking God for what He wanted *me* to be – as a wife and otherwise. I found (under the Lord's guidance) that I was so blind, and so faulty in the heart department that I had *no business* thinking about what anyone did or didn't do – in particular, what my husband did or didn't do.

"To make an already long story short(er), the Lord went through both our lives, our marriage, our home, everything, so fast and in such power that my husband was saved, empowered by the Holy Spirit, and his drug-doing friends ran for the hills. The Lord found us a house, we stopped striving with each other, started having people in our home to study the Bible, and no one could believe we were the same two people.

"But there were a few stubborn problems: There were still tensions in our sex life; I still had a nagging sense of unforgiveness against alcoholics; my husband still felt guilty about all he had done, even though he knew God had forgiven him and he was dead to the things he had done before; and (in part because of these things, he tells me now) he hadn't taken his position as the spiritual head of the house.

"Now by this time I knew that God and Rick could settle any problem without me poking my nose in it, so I gave the care of our sex life over to God, and concentrated on working for Him, loving my husband, and keeping my own self in line.

"And to tell you the truth, after what we had been through, I would have been perfectly satisfied to live with those things. Outwardly there was no sign of trouble, and we were both growing steadily. I was so grateful to our Lord Jesus because of the change from marital disaster to a loving and relatively peaceful home, that I'd have *gladly* lived with the seemingly small things in our lives for any length of time.

"Then, one night, a brother in the Lord came to a home Bible study we were having and told Rick about your seminar the next day. He went, and when he got home that Saturday afternoon, I could hardly believe I was talking to the same man! He asked my forgiveness for not taking the spiritual leadership in our family and home Bible study meeting, and *took it*. He shared the principle of 'release' in forgiveness he had learned from you; I got on my knees and today I am free from the root of bitterness and unforgiveness against alcoholics. Rick is free from his leftover guilt about the things his former self had done, and new power began to flow through our lives.

"Brother Cole, that was enough to keep me shouting the Lordship of Jesus Christ with fresh joy, and turning handsprings for a long, long time to come. But there's more.

"You spoke to the men about oral sex. That problem was the very specific one that I had turned over to the Lord, and then only with insecurity. (I wasn't too sure that Jesus was in the business of straightening out people's sex lives – I'd never heard much about it. But I reasoned that He did, after all, create it –

He's infinitely compassionate, and He does love us, so I banked on that and turned it over anyhow.) I had not said one word about it, not to my husband or anyone else, except to Jesus.

"Sir, when my husband walked in and told me what had been said, and that he had asked the Lord's forgiveness, and was now asking mine, the infinite love of the Lord Jesus Christ was so real to me I'd have been on my knees worshipping Him in that same instant, had I not been caught up in my husband's arms."

The seminar she was referring to was one of our "men only" meetings where I simply told the men that whatever is not of faith is sin, and the marriage bed is undefiled. The Holy Spirit is our teacher, the Bible says, and I let the Holy Spirit minister to the men individually after I presented the basic Biblical truths. This man accepted what God ministered to his heart and reaped a huge reward in his relationship with his wife. But the problem today is that often men are trained merely to hear sermons, not to study the Word of God or heed His "still small voice" in their hearts.

But notice in this woman's letter where the change began.

It always begins in us.

Any change you desire in someone else must begin in you. If your wife has seemed to be the wrong one, and you the right one, humble yourself before the Lord merely to do what He asks you to do in faith, believing that He will take care of the rest.

Impatience is the tool of the flesh, misunderstanding is the tool of the devil.

For your sake, your wife's sake, your children's sake, for God's sake – be the man God created you to be. Don't be a counterfeit. Be genuine. Be real.

Be a man.

The contradiction in men's lives is never so apparent as when they walk into the bedroom at night with the attitude, "Wait here, Jesus, I'll be back in the morning."

The Holy of Holies is now tabernacled in the heart of man. It's why Jesus could promise, **I will never leave thee, nor forsake thee** (Heb. 13:5, KJV). His Spirit indwells you every moment of every day, at all times working for your good. God is with you in the workroom, boardroom, kitchen, and bedroom.

Sure, there are some women as addicted to lust even as men, and they need the same renewing of the spirit of the mind that a man does. Sure, there are some women who consider their ability to seduce a man as evidence of their being a conqueror of him. Sure, there are women who are frigid.

Many women have problems with sex, not because they don't recognize it as a legitimate ministry of theirs to their husband, but because of his lusts.

One of the aspects of the man's ministry as prophet, priest and king is the ability to meet his wife's needs. Because a husband doesn't listen, a wife won't talk – about her problems – to him. But she will find someone who will listen, and when she does, she will often transfer her affection. That spells trouble.

That is why it is so important to understand the methods of communicating. Listening is the basic part of communication. You don't make a success in life because of your ability to speak, but because of your ability to listen.

Yes, God made sex good.

Righteousness makes it good.

Every man needs to have his heart and mind circumcised from uncleanness, to put away the impurities, and then to accept the riches of what is godly, pure and holy.

Sometimes it takes more than one effort to achieve excellence. That's why I wrote in the book *COURAGE: A Book for Champions* that "champions are not men who never fail, but men who never quit."

Like any investment, it will take time to see the results. Whereas the weak, fearful man gives up before the return comes in, a man who truly loves God will remain faithful until he reaps a harvest.

WHEN YOU FACE SEXUAL
TEMPTATION SCRIPTURES

But you are a shield around me, O Lord; you bestow glory on me and lift up my head.

Psalm 3:3

May integrity and uprightness protect me, because my hope is in you.

Psalm 25:21

Vindicate me, O Lord, for I have led a blameless life; I have trusted in the Lord without wavering.

But I lead a blameless life; redeem me and be merciful to me.

Psalm 26:1,11

Be pleased, O Lord, to save me; O Lord, come quickly to help me.

May all who seek to take my life be put to shame and confusion; may all who desire my ruin be turned back in disgrace.

Psalm 40:13,14

It is better to take refuge in the Lord than to trust in man.

Psalm 118:8

I have hidden your word in my heart that I might not sin against you.

Psalm 119:11

For the Lord gives wisdom, and from his mouth come knowledge and understanding.

He holds victory in store for the upright, he is a shield to those whose walk is blameless,

For he guards the course of the just and protects the way of his faithful ones.

Then you will understand what is right and just and fair – every good path.

For wisdom will enter your heart, and knowledge will be pleasant to your soul.

Discretion will protect you, and understanding will guard you.

It will save you also from the adulteress, from the wayward wife with her seductive words,

Who has left the partner of her youth and ignored the covenant she made before God.

For her house leads down to death and her paths to the spirits of the dead.

None who go to her return or attain the paths of life.

Thus you will walk in the ways of good men and keep to the paths of the righteous.

Proverbs 2:6-11,16-20

For the Lord will be your confidence and will keep your foot from being snared.

Proverbs 3:26

Drink water from your own cistern, running water from your own well.

Should your springs overflow in the streets, your streams of water in the public squares?

Let them be yours alone, never to be shared with strangers.

May your fountain be blessed, and may you rejoice in the wife of your youth.

A loving doe, a graceful deer – may her breasts satisfy you always, may you ever be captivated by her love.

Why be captivated, my son, by an adulteress? Why embrace the bosom of another man's wife?

For a man's ways are in full view of the Lord, and he examines all his paths.

The evil deeds of a wicked man ensnare him; the cords of his sin hold him fast.

He will die for lack of discipline, led astray by his own great folly.

Proverbs 5:15-23

For these [God's] commands are a lamp, this teaching is a light, and the corrections of discipline are the way to life,

Keeping you from the immoral woman, from the smooth tongue of the wayward wife.

Do not lust in your heart after her beauty or let her captivate you with her eyes,

For the prostitute reduces you to a loaf of bread, and the adulteress preys upon your very life.

Can a man scoop fire into his lap without his clothes being burned?

Can a man walk on hot coals without his feet being scorched?

So is he who sleeps with another man's wife; no one who touches her will go unpunished.

Proverbs 6:23-29

And lead us not into temptation, but deliver us from the evil one.

Matthew 6:13

Watch and pray so that you will not fall into temptation. The spirit is willing, but the body is weak.

Matthew 26:41

For sin shall not be your master, because you are not under law, but under grace.

Romans 6:14

No temptation has seized you except what is common to man. And God is faithful; he will not let you be tempted beyond what you can bear. But when you are tempted, he will also provide a way out so that you can stand up under it.

1 Corinthians 10:13

You were taught, with regard to your former way of life, to put off your old self, which is being corrupted by its deceitful desires.

Ephesians 4:22

Because he himself suffered when he was tempted, he is able to help those who are being tempted.

Hebrews 2:18

Blessed is the man who perseveres under trial, because when he has stood the test, he will receive the crown of life that God has promised to those who love him. When tempted, no one should say, "God is tempting me." For God cannot be tempted by evil, nor does he tempt anyone; but each one is tempted when, by his own evil desire, he is dragged away and enticed.

James 1:12-14

Be self-controlled and alert. Your enemy the devil prowls around like a roaring lion looking for someone to devour.

Resist him, standing firm in the faith, because you know that your brothers throughout the world are undergoing the same kind of sufferings.

1 Peter 5:8,9

The Lord knows how to rescue godly men from trials and to hold the unrighteous for the day of judgment, while continuing their punishment.

2 Peter 2:9

Since you have kept my command to endure patiently, I will also keep you from the hour of trial that is going to come upon the whole world to test those who live on the earth.

Revelation 3:10

On reaching the place, he said to them, "Pray that you will not fall into temptation."

"Why are you sleeping?" he asked them. "Get up and pray so that you will not fall into temptation."

Luke 22:40,46

For we do not have a high priest who is unable to sympathize with our weaknesses, but we have one who has been tempted in every way, just as we are – yet was without sin.

Hebrews 4:15

"Christians, we have been living far beneath our privileges in Christ. Ours should be an abundant life, with all the good things that flow from Calvary. God has given us these things to enjoy now. The idea that we have to wait until we go to heaven to enjoy God's goodness and mercy is a trick of the devil to cheat us out of the things that are ours. God is a God of the now! I AM is His Name!"

R.W. Schambach

STRENGTH FOR FATHERS

OTHER TOPICS AND SCRIPTURES TO STRENGTHEN THE SPIRIT-FILLED FATHER

When You Need Peace

will grant peace in the land, and you will lie down and no one will make you afraid. I will remove savage beasts from the land, and the sword will not pass through your country.

Leviticus 26:6

You will keep in perfect peace him whose mind is steadfast, because he trusts in you.

Isaiah 26:3

I will lie down and sleep in peace, for you alone, O Lord, make me dwell in safety.

Psalm 4:8

The Lord gives strength to his people; the Lord blesses his people with peace.

Psalm 29:11

Whom have I in heaven but you? And earth has nothing I desire besides you.
My flesh and my heart may fail, but God is the strength of my heart and my portion forever.

Psalm 73:25,26

Now may the Lord of peace himself give you peace at all times and in every way. The Lord be with all of you.

2 Thessalonians 3:16

Great peace have they who love your law, and nothing can make them stumble.

Psalm 119:165

I will listen to what God the Lord will say; he promises peace to his people, his saints.

Psalm 85:8a

Nevertheless, I will bring health and healing to it; I will heal my people and will let them enjoy abundant peace and security.

Jeremiah 33:6

Glory to God in the highest, and on earth peace to men on whom his favor rests.

Luke 2:14

On the evening of that first day of the week, when the disciples were together, with the doors locked for fear of the Jews, Jesus came and stood among them and said, "Peace be with you!"

John 20:19

Peace I leave with you; my peace I give you. I do not give to you as the world gives. Do not let your hearts be troubled and do not be afraid.

John 14:27

Therefore, since we have been justified through faith, we have peace with God through our Lord Jesus Christ.

Romans 5:1

For the kingdom of God is not a matter of eating and drinking, but of righteousness, peace and joy in the Holy Spirit.

Romans 14:17

May the God of hope fill you with all joy and peace as you trust in him, so that you may overflow with hope by the power of the Holy Spirit.

Romans 15:13

Do not be anxious about anything, but in everything, by prayer and petition, with thanksgiving, present your requests to God.

And the peace of God, which transcends all understanding, will guard your hearts and your minds in Christ Jesus.

Philippians 4:6,7

Let the peace of Christ rule in your hearts, since as members of one body you were called to peace. And be thankful.

Colossians 3:15

I have told you these things, so that in me you may have peace. In this world you will have trouble. But take heart! I have overcome the world.

John 16:33

WHEN YOU NEED HEALING

Surely he took up our infirmities and carried our sorrows, yet we considered him stricken by God, smitten by him, and afflicted.

But he was pierced for our transgressions, he was crushed for our iniquities; the punishment that brought us peace was upon him, and by his wounds we are healed.

Isaiah 53:4,5

Praise the Lord, O my soul, and forget not all his benefits –
Who forgives all your sins and heals all your diseases.

Psalm 103:2,3

He said, "If you listen carefully to the voice of the Lord your God and do what is right in his eyes, if you pay attention to his commands and keep all his decrees, I will not bring on you any of the diseases I brought on the Egyptians, for I am the Lord, who heals you."

Exodus 15:26

Jesus went throughout Galilee, teaching in their synagogues, preaching the good news of the kingdom, and healing every disease and sickness among the people.

Matthew 4:23

Jesus went through all the towns and villages, teaching in their synagogues, preaching the good news of the kingdom and healing every disease and sickness.

Matthew 9:35

But for you who revere my name, the sun of righteousness will rise with healing in its wings. And you will go out and leap like calves released from the stall.

Malachi 4:2

How God anointed Jesus of Nazareth with the Holy Spirit and power, and how he went around doing good and healing all who were under the power of the devil, because God was with him.

Acts 10:38

The Spirit of the Lord is on me, because he has anointed me to preach good news to the poor. He has sent me to proclaim freedom for the prisoners and recovery of sight for the blind, to release the oppressed.

Luke 4:18

He sent forth his word and healed them; he rescued them from the grave.

Psalm 107:20

The centurion replied, "Lord, I do not deserve to have you come under my roof. But just say the word, and my servant will be healed.

"For I myself am a man under authority, with soldiers under me. I tell this one, 'Go,' and he goes; and that one, 'Come,' and he comes. I say to my servant, 'Do this,' and he does it."

When Jesus heard this, he was astonished and said to those following him, "I tell you the truth, I have not found anyone in Israel with such great faith.

"I say to you that many will come from the east and the west, and will take their places at the feast with Abraham, Isaac and Jacob in the kingdom of heaven.

"But the subjects of the kingdom will be thrown outside, into the darkness, where there will be weeping and gnashing of teeth."

Then Jesus said to the centurion, "Go! It will be done just as you believed it would." And his servant was healed at that very hour.

When Jesus came into Peter's house, he saw Peter's mother-in-law lying in bed with a fever.

He touched her hand and the fever left her, and she got up and began to wait on him.

When evening came, many who were demon-possessed were brought to him, and he drove out the spirits with a word and healed all the sick.

Matthew 8:8-16

My son, pay attention to what I say; listen closely to my words.
Do not let them out of your sight, keep them within your heart;
For they are life to those who find them and health to a man's whole body.

Proverbs 4:20-22

A cheerful heart is good medicine, but a crushed spirit dries up the bones.

Proverbs 17:22

Dear friend, I pray that you may enjoy good health and that all may go well with you, even as your soul is getting along well.

3 John 2

When Jesus landed and saw a large crowd, he had compassion on them and healed their sick.

Matthew 14:14

And Jesus healed many who had various diseases. He also drove out many demons, but he would not let the demons speak because they knew who he was.

Mark 1:34

Therefore confess your sins to each other and pray for each other so that you may be healed. The prayer of a righteous man is powerful and effective.

James 5:16

He Himself bore our sins in his body on the tree, so that we might die to sins and live for righteousness; by his wounds you have been healed.

1 Peter 2:24

And these signs will accompany those who believe: In my name they will drive out demons; they will speak in new tongues;

They will pick up snakes with their hands; and when they drink deadly poison, it will not hurt them at all; they will place their hands on sick people, and they will get well.

Mark 16:17,18

WHEN YOU NEED WISDOM

God gave Solomon wisdom and very great insight, and a breadth of understanding as measureless as the sand on the seashore.

Solomon's wisdom was greater than the wisdom of all the men of the East, and greater than all the wisdom of Egypt.

He was wiser than any other man, including Ethan the Ezrahite – wiser than Herman, Calcol and Darda, the sons of Mahol. And his fame spread to all the surrounding nations.

He spoke three thousand proverbs and his songs numbered a thousand and five.

He described plant life, from the cedar of Lebanon to the hyssop that grows out of walls. He also taught about animals and birds, reptiles and fish.

Men of all nations came to listen to Solomon's wisdom, sent by all the kings of the world, who had heard of his wisdom.

1 Kings 4:29-34

The Lord gave Solomon wisdom, just as he had promised him. There were peaceful relations between Hiram and Solomon, and the two of them made a treaty.

1 Kings 5:12

May the Lord give you discretion and understanding when he puts you in command over Israel, so that you may keep the law of the Lord your God.

1 Chronicles 22:12

Surely you desire truth in the inner parts; you teach me wisdom in the inmost place.

Psalm 51:6

Teach us to number our days aright, that we may gain a heart of wisdom.

Psalm 90:12

For attaining wisdom and discipline; for understanding words of insight.

Proverbs 1:2

The fear of the Lord is the beginning of wisdom; all who follow his precepts have good understanding. To him belongs eternal praise.

Psalm 111:10

Turning your ear to wisdom and applying your heart to understanding,
And if you call out for insight and cry aloud for understanding,
And if you look for it as for silver and search for it as for hidden treasure,
Then you will understand the fear of the Lord and find the knowledge of God.

For the Lord gives wisdom, and from his mouth come knowledge and understanding.

He holds victory in store for the upright, he is a shield to those whose walk is blameless.

Proverbs 2:2-7

Blessed is the man who finds wisdom, the man who gains understanding.
Proverbs 3:13

Wisdom is supreme; therefore get wisdom. Though it cost all you have, get understanding.

I guide you in the way of wisdom and lead you along straight paths.
Proverbs 4:7,11

For wisdom is more precious than rubies, and nothing you desire can compare with her.

I, wisdom, dwell together with prudence; I possess knowledge and discretion.

Proverbs 8:11,12

How much better to get wisdom than gold, to choose understanding rather than silver!

Proverbs 16:16

He who gets wisdom loves his own soul; he who cherishes understanding prospers.

Proverbs 19:8

And the child grew and became strong; he was filled with wisdom, and the grace of God was upon him.

Luke 2:40

But to those whom God has called, both Jews and Greeks, Christ the power of God and the wisdom of God.

For the foolishness of God is wiser than man's wisdom, and the weakness of God is stronger than man's strength.

1 Corinthians 1:24,25

We do, however, speak a message of wisdom among the mature, but not the wisdom of this age or of the rulers of this age, who are coming to nothing.

1 Corinthians 2:6

For the wisdom of this world is foolishness in God's sight. As it is written: "He catches the wise in their craftiness."

1 Corinthians 3:19

That he lavished on us with all wisdom and understanding.
I keep asking that the God of our Lord Jesus Christ, the glorious Father, may give you the Spirit of wisdom and revelation, so that you may know him better.

Ephesians 1:8,17

For this reason, since the day we heard about you, we have not stopped praying for you and asking God to fill you with the knowledge of his will through all spiritual wisdom and understanding.

Colossians 1:9

Let the word of Christ dwell in you richly as you teach and admonish one another with all wisdom, and as you sing psalms, hymns and spiritual songs with gratitude in your hearts to God.

Colossians 3:16

If any of you lacks wisdom, he should ask God, who gives generously to all without finding fault, and it will be given to him.

James 1:5

WHEN YOU NEED JOY

For his anger lasts only a moment, but his favor lasts a lifetime; weeping may remain for a night, but rejoicing comes in the morning.

Psalm 30:5

Rejoice in the Lord and be glad, you righteous; sing, all you who are upright in heart!

Psalm 32:11

But may all who seek you rejoice and be glad in you; may those who love your salvation always say, "The Lord be exalted!"

Psalm 40:16

Shout for joy to the Lord, all the earth.
Worship the Lord with gladness; come before him with joyful songs.

Psalm 100:1,2

Those who sow in tears will reap with songs of joy.
He who goes about weeping, carrying seed to sow, will return with songs of joy, carrying sheaves with him.

Psalm 126:5,6

Nehemiah said, "Go and enjoy choice food and sweet drinks, and send some to those who have nothing prepared. This day is sacred to our Lord. Do not grieve, for the joy of the Lord is your strength."

Nehemiah 8:10

Be joyful always.

1 Thessalonians 5:16

Is any one of you in trouble? He should pray. Is anyone happy? Let him sing songs of praise.

James 5:13

I have told you this so that my joy may be in you and that your joy may be complete.

John 15:11

Until now you have not asked for anything in my name. Ask and you will receive, and your joy will be complete.
I told you these things, so that in me you may have peace. In this world you will have trouble. But take heart! I have overcome the world.

John 16:24,33

I am coming to you now, but I say these things while I am still in the world, so that they may have the full measure of my joy within them.

John 17:13

You have made known to me the paths of life; you will fill me with joy in your presence.

Acts 2:28

For the kingdom of God is not a matter of eating and drinking, but of righteousness, peace and joy in the Holy Spirit.

Romans 14:17

May the God of hope fill you with all joy and peace as you trust in him, so that you may overflow with hope by the power of the Holy Spirit.

Romans 15:13

But the fruit of the Spirit is love, joy, peace, patience, kindness, goodness, faithfulness, gentleness and self-control.

Galatians 5:22,23

Rejoice in the Lord always. I will say it again: Rejoice!

Philippians 4:4

Though you have not seen him, you love him; and even though you do not see him now, you believe in him and are filled with an inexpressible and glorious joy.

1 Peter 1:8

WHEN YOU NEED PATIENCE

Not only so, but we also rejoice in our sufferings, because we know that suffering produces perseverance;
Perseverance, character; and character, hope.

Romans 5:3,4

May the God who gives endurance and encouragement give you a spirit of unity among yourselves as you follow Christ Jesus.

Romans 15:5

But if we hope for what we do not yet have, we wait for it patiently.

Romans 8:25

You, however, know all about my teaching, my way of life, my purpose, faith, patience, love, endurance.

2 Timothy 3:10

But you, man of God, flee from all this, and pursue righteousness, godliness, faith, love, endurance and gentleness.

1 Timothy 6:11

Teach the older men to be temperate, worthy of respect, self-controlled, and sound in faith, in love and in endurance.

Titus 2:2

We do not want you to become lazy, but to imitate those who through faith and patience inherit what has been promised.

Hebrews 6:12

You need to persevere so that when you have done the will of God, you will receive what he has promised.

Hebrews 10:36

Therefore, since we are surrounded by such a great cloud of witnesses, let us throw off everything that hinders and the sin that so easily entangles, and let us run with perseverance the race marked out for us.

Hebrews 12:1

Because you know that the testing of your faith develops perseverance.

James 1:3

For this very reason, make every effort to add to your faith goodness; and to goodness, knowledge;
And to knowledge, self-control; and to self-control, perseverance; and to perseverance, godliness.

2 Peter 1:5,6

Since you have kept my command to endure patiently, I will also keep you from the hour of trial that is going to come upon the whole world to test those who live on the earth.

Revelation 3:10

WHEN YOU NEED FAVOR

No one will be able to stand up against you all the days of your life. As I was with Moses, so I will be with you; I will never leave you nor forsake you.

Joshua 1:5

For surely, O Lord, you bless the righteous; you surround them with your favor as with a shield.

Psalm 5:12

If the Lord delights in a man's way, he makes his steps firm.

Psalm 37:23

Then you will win favor and a good name in the sight of God and man.

Proverbs 3:4

For whoever finds me finds life and receives favor from the Lord.

Proverbs 8:35

A good man obtains favor from the Lord, but the Lord condemns a crafty man.

Proverbs 12:2

Fools mock at making amends for sin, but goodwill is found among the upright.

Proverbs 14:9

Foreigners will rebuild your walls, and their kings will serve you. Though in anger I struck you, in favor I will show you compassion.

Isaiah 60:10

The angel went to her and said, "Greetings, you who are highly favored! The Lord is with you."

Mary was greatly troubled at his words and wondered what kind of greeting this might be.

But the angel said to her, "Do not be afraid, Mary, you have found favor with God."

Luke 1:28-30

Let us then approach the throne of grace with confidence, so that we may receive mercy and find grace to help us in our time of need.

Hebrews 4:16

But you are a chosen people, a royal priesthood, a holy nation, a people belonging to God, that you may declare the praises of him who called you out of darkness into his wonderful light.

1 Peter 2:9

Mordecai had a cousin named Hadassah, whom he had brought up because she had neither father nor mother. This girl, who was also known as Esther, was lovely in form and features, and Mordecai had taken her as his own daughter when her father and mother died.

When the turn came for Esther (the girl Mordecai had adopted, the daughter of his uncle Abihail) to go to the king, she asked for nothing other than what Hegai, the king's eunuch who was in charge of the harem, suggested. And Esther won the favor of everyone who saw her.

Esther 2:7,15

Then Queen Esther answered, "If I have found favor with you, O king, and if it pleases your majesty, grant me my life – this is my petition. And spare my people – this is my request."

Esther 7:3

"If it pleases the king," she said, "and if he regards me with favor and thinks it the right thing to do, and if he is pleased with me, let an order be written overruling the dispatches that Haman son of Hammedatha, the Agagite, devised and wrote to destroy the Jews in all the king's provinces."

Esther 8:5

WHEN YOU NEED COMFORT

The eternal God is your refuge, and underneath are the everlasting arms. He will drive out your enemy before you, saying, "Destroy him!"

Deuteronomy 33:27

Even though I walk through the valley of the shadow of death, I will fear no evil, for you are with me; your rod and your staff, they comfort me.

Psalm 23:4

For in the day of trouble he will keep me safe in his dwelling; he will hide me in the shelter of his tabernacle and set me high upon a rock.

Psalm 27:5

I will extol the Lord at all times; his praise will always be on my lips.
My soul will boast in the Lord; let the afflicted hear and rejoice.

Glorify the Lord with me; let us exalt his name together.

I sought the Lord, and he answered me; he delivered me from all my fears.

Those who look to him are radiant; their faces are never covered with shame.

This poor man called, and the Lord heard him; he saved him out of all his troubles.

The angel of the Lord encamps around those who fear him, and he delivers them.

Taste and see that the Lord is good; blessed is the man who takes refuge in him.

Fear the Lord, you his saints, for those who fear him lack nothing.

Psalm 34:1-9

God is our refuge and strength, an ever-present help in trouble.

Psalm 46:1

And call upon me in the day of trouble; I will deliver you, and you will honor me.

Psalm 50:15

Cast your cares on the Lord and he will sustain you; he will never let the righteous fall.

Psalm 55:22

Even in darkness light dawns for the upright, for the gracious and compassionate and righteous man.

Psalm 112:4

Praise be to the God and Father of our Lord Jesus Christ, the Father of compassion and the God of all comfort,

Who comforts us in all our troubles, so that we can comfort those in any trouble with the comfort we ourselves have received from God.

2 Corinthians 1:3,4

We are hard pressed on every side, but not crushed; perplexed, but not in despair;

Persecuted, but not abandoned; struck down, but not destroyed.

2 Corinthians 4:8,9

He heals the brokenhearted and binds up their wounds.

Psalm 147:3

So do not fear, for I am with you; do not be dismayed, for I am your God. I will strengthen you and help you; I will uphold you with my righteous right hand.

Isaiah 41:10

When you pass through the waters, I will be with you; and when you pass through the rivers, they will not sweep over you. When you walk through the fire, you will not be burned; the flames will not set you ablaze.

Isaiah 43:2

The Lord is good, a refuge in times of trouble. He cares for those who trust in him.

Nahum 1:7

Blessed are those who mourn, for they will be comforted.

Matthew 5:4

Come to me, all you who are weary and burdened, and I will give you rest.

Matthew 11:28

Do not let your hearts be troubled. Trust in God; trust also in me.
And I will ask the Father, and he will give you another Counselor to be with you forever –
I will not leave you as orphans; I will come to you.

John 14:1,16,18

Peace I leave with you; my peace I give you. I do not give to you as the world gives. Do not let your hearts be troubled and do not be afraid.

John 14:27

Carry each other's burdens, and in this way you will fulfill the law of Christ.

Galatians 6:2

WHEN YOU NEED PROTECTION

He who dwells in the shelter of the Most High will rest in the shadow of the Almighty.

I will say of the Lord, "He is my refuge and my fortress, my God, in whom I trust."

Surely he will save you from the fowler's snare and from the deadly pestilence.

A thousand may fall at your side, ten thousand at your right hand, but it will not come near you.

Then no harm will befall you, no disaster will come near your tent.

"Because he loves me," says the Lord, "I will rescue him; I will protect him, for he acknowledges my name.

"He will call upon me, and I will answer him; I will be with him in trouble, I will deliver him and honor him."

Psalm 91:1-3,7,10,14,15

The angel of the Lord encamps around those who fear him, and he delivers them.

Psalm 34:7

You are my hiding place; you will protect me from trouble and surround me with songs of deliverance. *Selah*

Psalm 32:7

Even though I walk through the valley of the shadow of death, I will fear no evil, for you are with me; your rod and your staff, they comfort me.

Psalm 23:4

For the eyes of the Lord range throughout the earth to strengthen those whose hearts are fully committed to him.

2 Chronicles 16:9

He said: "Listen, King Jehoshaphat and all who live in Judah and Jerusalem! This is what the Lord says to you: 'Do not be afraid or discouraged because of this vast army. For the battle is not yours, but God's.'

"You will not have to fight this battle. Take up your positions; stand firm and see the deliverance the Lord will give you, O Judah and Jerusalem. Do not be afraid; do not be discouraged. Go out to face them tomorrow, and the Lord will be with you."

2 Chronicles 20:15,17

As the mountains surround Jerusalem, so the Lord surrounds his people both now and forevermore.

Psalm 125:2

Have you not put a hedge around him and his household and everything he has? You have blessed the work of his hands, so that his flocks and herds are spread throughout the land.

Job 1:10

The Lord your God, who is going before you, will fight for you, as he did for you in Egypt, before your very eyes.

Deuteronomy 1:30

He rescued me from my powerful enemy, from my foes, who were too strong for me.

Psalm 18:17

For you have been my refuge, a strong tower against the foe.

Psalm 61:3

When you lie down, you will not be afraid; when you lie down, your sleep will be sweet.

Proverbs 3:24

When you pass through the waters, I will be with you; and when you pass through the rivers, they will not sweep over you. When you walk through the fire, you will not be burned; the flames will not set you ablaze.

Isaiah 43:2

WHEN YOU NEED FAITH

I tell you the truth, if anyone says to this mountain, "Go, throw yourself into the sea," and does not doubt in his heart but believes that what he says will happen, it will be done for him.

Therefore I tell you, whatever you ask for in prayer, believe that you have received it, and it will be yours.

Mark 11:23,24

Yet he did not waver through unbelief regarding the promise of God, but was strengthened in his faith and gave glory to God,

Being fully persuaded that God had power to do what he had promised.

Romans 4:20,21

So that your faith might not rest on men's wisdom, but on God's power.

1 Corinthians 2:5

But what does it say? "The word is near you; it is in your mouth and in your heart," that is, the word of faith we are proclaiming.

Consequently, faith comes from hearing the message, and the message is heard through the word of Christ.

Romans 10:8,17

Clearly no one is justified before God by the law, because, "The righteous will live by faith."

Galatians 3:11

In addition to all this, take up the shield of faith, with which you can extinguish all the flaming arrows of the evil one.

Ephesians 6:16

So do not throw away your confidence; it will be richly rewarded.
But my righteous one will live by faith. And if he shrinks back, I will not be pleased with him.

Hebrews 10:35,38

Now faith is being sure of what we hope for and certain of what we do not see.
And without faith it is impossible to please God, because anyone who comes to him must believe that he exists and that he rewards those who earnestly seek him.

Hebrews 11:1,6

But when he asks, he must believe and not doubt, because he who doubts is like a wave of the sea, blown and tossed by the wind.

James 1:6

For everyone born of God overcomes the world. This is the victory that has overcome the world, even our faith.

1 John 5:4

Are they not the ones who are slandering the noble name of him to whom you belong?
What good is it, my brothers, if a man claims to have faith but has no deeds? Can such faith save him?
You foolish man, do you want evidence that faith without deeds is useless?

James 2:7,14,20

"Prayer must become as natural as breathing. With such prayer, men defeat spiritual forces arrayed against them that no human means could overcome."

Gordon Lindsay

PERSONAL PRAYERS

PRAYER FOR SPOUSE

Father, I thank You for my mate who delights herself in You. Your Spirit rests upon her – the Spirit of wisdom and understanding, the Spirit of counsel and power; the Spirit of knowledge and the fear of the Lord.

Thank You, Father, that my mate is loving, patient and kind. She is not envious, boastful, proud, rude, or self-seeking. She is not easily angered and never keeps a record of my wrongs. She is quick to forgive. She rejoices when righteousness and truth prevail.

She always protects me, speaks well of me and believes the best of me. She always hopes and perseveres because You, Lord, are her primary focus.

Father, because we love You first and foremost and are submitted to You as the Head of the Church, we are committed and submitted to one another, daily maturing in the oneness You meant to exist in our relationship.

In my mate's tongue is life and not death. She strengthens our relationship by speaking Your Word, Lord, in the face of any circumstance. She is never degrading or intimidating, but always uplifts, edifies and encourages.

Thank You, Father, that my mate is a peacemaker. She refuses to allow strife, envy, or selfishness in our marriage and home. Because our home is a haven of love, peace and harmony, our prayers are not hindered and Your blessings are overtaking us, Lord.

Thank You, Father, for helping us to mature in You and in our relationship with one another. Amen.

Scripture References:

Ephesians 5:22-33
Psalm 37:4
Mark 11:23-25
Proverbs 18:21
James 3:16-18
1 Peter 3:7

Isaiah 11:2
1 Corinthians 13:4-8
Isaiah 1:19
Matthew 5:9
Psalm 133:1-3

PRAYER FOR CHILDREN

Thank You, Father, that our children are a heritage and a reward from You. Before You formed them in the womb, You knew each child. You knit each child together in the womb fearfully and wonderfully, Lord.

Your thoughts and plans for our children are blessed. You created them to be signs and wonders in the earth.

Our children are taught of You, Lord, and great is their peace.

No weapon formed against our children shall prosper, Lord Jesus. Wrong relationships cannot prevail, because they hunger and thirst for Your righteousness, Lord. Wrong thoughts cannot prevail in our children, because they have the mind of Christ. Lies and deception cannot prosper against them or take residence in them, because they are dominated by Your truth, Lord. Greater is He who is in them than he who is in the world.

No sickness or disease can prosper against our children, Lord, because they have been redeemed from the curse of the law, and by Your stripes, Lord Jesus, they have already been healed.

It is well with our children, because they are respectful and obedient to their parents and to all who are in authority over them in Jesus' name.

Your shed blood, Lord Jesus, cleanses and protects our children – spirit, soul (which includes mind, will, emotions and intellect) and body.

Thank You, Father, that You are perfecting everything that concerns our children. They will do great exploits for You, Father, in Jesus' name. Amen.

Scripture References:

Psalm 127:3-5	Jeremiah 1:5
Psalm 139:13-18	Jeremiah 29:11
Isaiah 8:18, KJV	Isaiah 54:13,17
Proverbs 11:21	Matthew 5:6
1 Corinthians 2:16	1 John 4:4
Galatians 3:13,14	1 Peter 2:24
Ephesians 6:1-3	Psalm 138:8
Daniel 11:32b	

PRAYER FOR HEALTH AND HEALING

We accept You, Father, as Jehovah Rapha, our Healer, for You said, "I am the Lord Who heals you." We accept Jesus' completed work at Calvary, which includes full payment for our sicknesses and diseases, as well as our sins, poverty and spiritual death.

For existing symptoms, sicknesses and diseases, Lord, we rise up in the authority You have invested in us and we agree with Your Word, "Nothing will harm us."

You said in Your Word, Lord, to decree a thing and it would be so. We decree that sickness and disease cannot come near our dwelling, for Your divine health resides in us, O Lord.

Father, we receive the promise of Your Word that though the righteous face many afflictions, which could include sickness, disease and/or symptoms, *You will deliver us from them all!*

Because we revere Your name, Lord Jesus, the Sun of Righteousness will arise in our behalf with healing in His wings. We will go forth totally whole, leaping as calves loosed from their stalls, with rejoicing in our hearts.

In You, Lord Jesus, we will run through enemy troops and leap over enemy walls! Nothing shall be impossible to us that is ordained of You, because we have Your vitality, Lord Jesus! We will not be hindered from fulfilling Your purposes for our lives, Lord, because we live and move and have our total being, including health and healing, in You! Amen.

Scripture References:

Job 22:28, KJV
Exodus 15:26
Luke 10:19
Psalm 34:19
Acts 17:28
Proverbs 17:22

Malachi 4:2, AMP
1 Peter 2:24
Psalm 91:10-16
Matthew 8:17
Psalm 18:29

PRAYER FOR FINANCES

Heavenly Father, thank You that You teach us how to profit and lead us in the way we should go.

As born-again believers, Lord, we thank You that our covenant agreement with You includes provision for all of our needs. It includes an exchange of our lack for Your prosperity, Lord, not only in finances, but in every area of life.

We speak to the mountain of financial lack, Lord, and command it to be removed from our lives and replaced with the finances from heaven, which are loosed as we bring our tithes and offerings into Your storehouse. We decree financial increase, Lord, not just to bless us, but so we can bless others with the Good News of You, Lord Jesus, as well as meet their practical needs of food, clothing and shelter.

We decree that we are the head and not the tail, above and not beneath, blessed coming and going and abounding in our checking and saving accounts.

Thank You for the abundant life we have in You, Lord Jesus. We command that the devil restore seven-fold, in Jesus' name, for anything he has taken from us.

We loose the wealth of the wicked to come into our hands, Lord, so we can complete Your plans upon the earth.

Thank You, Father, that in Christ Jesus, we are prosperous in our finances, in health and in well-being, just as our soul prospers by daily input of and meditation upon Your Word, Lord. Amen.

Scripture References:

Isaiah 48:17, AMP	Philippians 4:19
Proverbs 13:22, KJV	Mark 11:23,24
Job 22:28	Deuteronomy 28:1-14
Malachi 3:8-12	Psalm 115:14,15
Psalm 41:1,2	John 10:10
3 John 2, KJV	Joshua 1:8

PRAYER FOR SAFETY AND PROTECTION

Father, we decree safety over our lives and over the lives of our seed (our children) – spirit, soul, body and property – because of the shed blood of Your Son, Jesus Christ.

We dwell in the shelter of the Most High and rest in His shadow. You, Lord, are our refuge and fortress, and we trust in You.

Thank You for protecting us from the devil's traps and snares, Lord, and for covering us with Your feathers. We take refuge under Your wings, and Your faithfulness is a shield to us. Thank You, Lord, that You give Your angels charge over us to keep us in all of our ways.

We will not fear, for You are not only our dwelling, but our Source of everything for our lives, Lord, including safety and protection.

It is a covenant promise to Your children, Lord, that if we love and acknowledge You, not just with lip service but from our hearts, You will protect us, deliver us, honor us and give us long life.

Thank You for the armor of protection You have given us, Lord – the belt of truth; the breastplate of righteousness; the gospel of peace for our feet; the shield of faith to extinguish all the flaming arrows of the devil; the helmet of salvation; the sword of the Spirit, which is Your Word; and prayer in the Spirit with all kinds of prayer.

We shall not be destroyed by any plot or scheme of the devil, Lord, for we are knowledgeable of Your Word. As we resist the devil with Your Word, he flees from us in great terror! Greater is He who is in us than he who is in the world.

Thank You, Lord, for divine safety and protection over our spirit, our mind, will, emotions and intellect, over our bodies and over the provision and possessions You have given us. Amen.

Scripture References:

Revelation 12:11

Psalm 91:1-16

Hosea 4:6

1 John 4:4

Job 22:28, KJV

Matthew 18:19,20

James 4:7

Ephesians 6:10-18

"The Christian home is the greatest testimony and the greatest strength to the Christian community today. You husbands, be men. Do not be dictators and bosses. Be lovers. Be somebody who will build up, guide and guard and protect your wife. Make her proud of you."

John Osteen

PEACE AND HARMONY
IN THE HOME

"HEAVEN ON EARTH IN YOUR HOME AND MARRIAGE"

BY KENNETH & GLORIA COPELAND

L iving in a home filled with the love and peace of God Himself is almost like living in heaven right here on earth.

We all know that's true. And we all long to live in such a home. Yet time and again, we shortchange our families. We spend our kindest words and our most winning smiles on those beyond our front door. Despite our best intentions, we fall prey to temptation, to selfishness, and impatience at home more often than anywhere else.

Have you ever wondered why?

The answer is simpler than you may suspect. Spiritually speaking, your family is under attack. You see, it is not only one of your most precious gifts, when it's operating in harmony, it's one of your most powerful resources. Satan knows that, even if you don't. And he's out to destroy it.

His battle plan is simple. He will do everything he can to create strife in your home. He'll stir up feelings of self-pity and jealousy. He'll encourage you to nurse resentments and harbor bitterness. And through it all, his purpose remains the same: to divide and destroy your home.

Why is he so terrified of your family living in harmony? Look at Matthew 18:19,20 (KJV) and you'll see. There Jesus says, **Again I say unto you, That if two of you shall agree on earth as touching any thing that they shall**

ask, it shall be done for them of my Father which is in heaven. For where two or three are gathered together in my name, there am I in the midst of them.

When God's people get in harmony with each other, miracles start to happen. Their agreement creates an atmosphere in which God's supernatural, miracle-working power is free to flow!

So Satan is constantly tempting us to spoil that atmosphere, to foul things up by being at odds with each other. And all too often we fall prey to his tactics simply because we don't realize just how dangerous strife really is. One close look at the Word of God will solve that problem, however. It says in no uncertain terms that strife is extremely dangerous business.

Second Timothy 2:26, for example, says that those who are in strife are taken captive by Satan at his will. James 3:16 (KJV) says **where envying and strife is, there is confusion and every evil work.**

That's how many Christian families are destroyed. They allow themselves the "luxury" of a few quarrels, a few disagreements without realizing they're offering Satan an open door into their home. And before they know it, he's tearing their lives apart.

How can you stop the destruction before it starts? Anchor yourself to God's Word. Find out what He has to say about the power of agreement. Stop looking at your marriage from your own limited human perspective and start seeing it as God sees it. That way you won't drift helplessly into an argument every time a gust of emotion blows through your home.

According to the Word of God, marriage is not an arrangement based on convenience or on emotion. It's a covenant between two people, each promising to give himself to the other in life and even in death if need be. It is so serious and so sacred that the New Testament frequently compares the relationship of the husband and wife to the relationship between Jesus and the Church.

Of the relationship between Christ and the Church, Ephesians 5:30 (KJV) says, **For we are members of his body, of his flesh, and of his bones.** And of the relationship between a man and his wife, Matthew 19:5 (KJV) says, **For this cause shall a man leave father and mother, and shall cleave to his wife: and they twain shall be one flesh.**

Just as the Church has been joined with Jesus in spirit to actually become His Body on the earth, so marriage partners are joined spiritually and physically to become "one flesh." The two relationships are so similar that one version of the Bible says that by rightly discerning the Body of Christ, you rightly discern the marriage union.

Are you beginning to see how powerful God intended the marriage relationship to be?

Now look again at Matthew 18:20 (KJV). It says, **where two or three are gathered together in my name, there am I in the midst of them.** If you and your spouse are both believers, you've been joined together in Jesus' name. Isn't that right? That means Jesus is there in the midst of you. Now all you two have to do is to agree on anything according to the Word of God, ask it, and it will be done for you. Jesus said so!

You don't have to be the victim of your circumstances! You don't have to sit around and let the devil steal your kids or your health or your money. If you'll just get in agreement and pray, you can run him right out of those areas of your life.

Read Matthew 18:19 (KJV) again. **If two of you shall agree on earth as touching any thing that they shall ask, it shall be done for them of my Father which is in heaven.** Meditate on that verse. Get a revelation of it! When you do, you won't be willing to throw away that kind of prayer power for the sake of some silly argument!

You'll also want to clean out your emotional closets and get rid of all the resentments you've stored up from the past. Why? Because those, too, will sap the power of your prayers. Follow the instructions of Jesus in Mark 11:25 (KJV). **And when ye stand praying, forgive, if ye have aught against any: that your Father also which is in heaven may forgive you your trespasses.**

Gloria and I know how important harmony is within our family. We endeavor to keep the power of agreement at work in our lives. We work at not allowing strife in our home. We both realize that it's more important to keep the peace than it is to prove that we're right and that helps us keep our conversations with each other in line.

Rather than being guided by our human wisdom, we must allow ourselves to be guided by the wisdom which is from above which, according to James 3:17 (AMP), is peace-loving, courteous, considerate, gentle, willing to yield to reason, and full of compassion. When we live in peace instead of strife, we are enjoying one of God's most powerful blessings – a love-ruled home.

You may say, "But Brother Copeland, you don't know my wife! She's the one who's causing all the problems. I've been praying that God would change her for 20 years."

Don't you worry about that. You concentrate on YOU! Start praying that God will turn you into the husband of her dreams. Wives, you start asking God to make you into the wife your husband really needs. You'll be amazed at the miracles that can come out of a prayer like that.

Once you get things straight between you and your husband or you and your wife, you'll have a lot more power where your children are concerned. In this day of crime, drugs, perversion, and rebellion running rampant, Christian parents all over this nation are concerned about their children. Yet very few of them know what rights and promises are given to them as parents in the Word of God.

Galatians 3:13,14 (KJV) says, **Christ hath redeemed us from the curse of the law, being made a curse for us: for it is written, Cursed is every one that hangeth on a tree: That the blessing of Abraham might come on the Gentiles through Jesus Christ; that we might receive the promise of the Spirit through faith.** For the most part, those of us who are believers have been well taught about our redemption from sin, sickness, disease, and poverty. We know we don't have to put up with those things. But often, when it comes to our children, we live with the curse as though we had no other choice.

What are the effects of that curse? You can find them in Deuteronomy 28:32 (KJV).

Thy sons and thy daughters shall be given unto another people, and thine eye shall look, and fail with longing for them all the day long: and there shall be no might in thine hand. And verse 41 says, **Thou shalt beget sons and daughters, but thou shalt not enjoy them; for they shall go into captivity.**

Many parents today are living out these verses. They're watching helplessly as their children are taken captive by the ways of the world. But it doesn't have to be that way. Jesus has broken the power of the curse in the life of every believer. Act on His promise. Order Satan out of your children's lives.

Don't wait for your children to make the first move. Go to battle for them in prayer. Children don't understand the unseen forces that come against them. Part of your responsibility as a parent is to put up a shield of faith that will help protect your children from the influence of the evil one.

Like most parents, Gloria and I have had to deal with rebellion. We realized that it had to be stopped and stopped quickly. When we first saw the warning signs, we sought for the scriptures we could use to combat these forces. Gloria made a study of them. She wrote down every scriptural promise that she could find concerning our children.

I'll never forget the day she and I sat down in the middle of the bed amidst a pile of papers and Bibles and agreed on those scriptures in prayer. We took authority in the spirit world and refused to give the devil any room to operate.

Once we exercised the authority given us by God's Word, we also took every opportunity to minister love to the children. Before long, they were responding to it. It wasn't easy, though. At times we wanted to cry or lose our tempers. But, whenever we were tempted to react in the natural, we would remember such scriptures as Jeremiah 31:16,17 (KJV). **Thus saith the Lord; Refrain thy voice from weeping, and thine eyes from tears: for thy work shall be rewarded, saith the Lord; and they** [your children] **shall come again from the land of the enemy. And there is hope in thine end, saith the Lord, that thy children shall come again to their own border.**

We stood on the promises of God, and those promises got the job done! They'll do the same for you. Take them to heart. Resist the temptation to weep for your children. Start believing the Word. It is the only thing that will bring them around. Second Peter 2:9 assures us that God knows how to deliver them, so give Him the opportunity. Do your part and trust Him to do His.

And above all, **as far as it depends on you, live at peace with everyone** (Rom. 12:18, AMP). Resist strife just as you would sin or sickness. Discord is deadly, and it is always of the devil. You can't afford it. It will paralyze the power of God in your life.

If you allow the enemy to stop you at your own front door, you will be no threat to him anywhere else. Decide today that disharmony, clashing, and tension are luxuries that you cannot afford – especially at home! Give your family one of the greatest gifts of all time – a home full of love, peace, and power of God. Then you can all enjoy a little bit of heaven on earth...all year around.

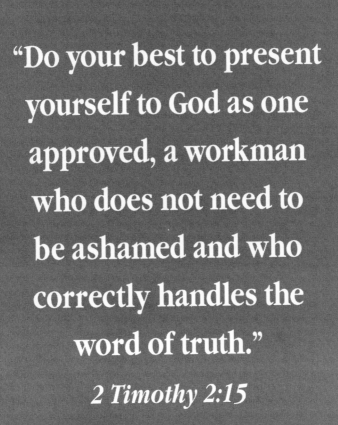

"Do your best to present yourself to God as one approved, a workman who does not need to be ashamed and who correctly handles the word of truth."

2 Timothy 2:15

SPIRITUAL ENRICHMENT

Read the Bible in One Year

JANUARY

1 Gen. 1-2; Ps.1; Matt. 1-2
2 Gen. 3-4; Ps. 2; Matt. 3-4
3 Gen. 5-7; Ps. 3; Matt. 5
4 Gen. 8-9; Ps. 4; Matt. 6-7
5 Gen. 10-11; Ps. 5; Matt. 8-9
6 Gen. 12-13; Ps. 6; Matt. 10-11
7 Gen. 14-15; Ps. 7; Matt. 12
8 Gen. 16-17; Ps. 8; Matt. 13
9 Gen. 18-19; Ps. 9; Matt. 14-15
10 Gen. 20-21; Ps. 10; Matt. 16-17
11 Gen. 22-23; Ps. 11; Matt. 18
12 Gen. 24; Ps. 12; Matt. 19-20
13 Gen. 25-26; Ps. 13; Matt. 21
14 Gen. 27-28; Ps. 14; Matt. 22
15 Gen. 29-30; Ps. 15; Matt. 23
16 Gen. 31-32; Ps. 16; Matt. 24
17 Gen. 33-34; Ps. 17; Matt. 25
18 Gen. 35-36; Ps. 18; Matt. 26
19 Gen. 37-38; Ps. 19; Matt. 27
20 Gen. 39-40; Ps. 20; Matt. 28
21 Gen. 41-42; Ps. 21; Mark 1
22 Gen. 43-44; Ps. 22; Mark 2
23 Gen. 45-46; Ps. 23; Mark 3
24 Gen. 47-48; Ps. 24; Mark 4
25 Gen. 49-50; Ps. 25; Mark 5
26 Ex. 1-2; Ps. 26; Mark 6
27 Ex. 3-4; Ps. 27; Mark 7
28 Ex. 5-6; Ps. 28; Mark 8
29 Ex. 7-8; Ps. 29; Mark 9
30 Ex. 9-10; Ps. 30; Mark 10
31 Ex. 11-12; Ps. 31; Mark 11

FEBRUARY

1 Ex. 13-14; Ps. 32; Mark 12
2 Ex. 15-16; Ps. 33; Mark 13
3 Ex. 17-18; Ps. 34; Mark 14
4 Ex. 19-20; Ps. 35; Mark 15
5 Ex. 21-22; Ps. 36; Mark 16
6 Ex. 23-24; Ps. 37; Luke 1
7 Ex. 25-26; Ps. 38; Luke 2
8 Ex. 27-28; Ps. 39; Luke 3
9 Ex. 29-30; Ps. 40; Luke 4
10 Ex. 31-32; Ps. 41; Luke 5
11 Ex. 33-34; Ps. 42; Luke 6
12 Ex. 35-36; Ps. 43; Luke 7
13 Ex. 37-38; Ps. 44; Luke 8
14 Ex. 39-40; Ps. 45; Luke 9
15 Lev. 1-2; Ps. 46; Luke 10
16 Lev. 3-4; Ps. 47; Luke 11
17 Lev. 5-6; Ps. 48; Luke 12
18 Lev. 7-8; Ps. 49; Luke 13
19 Lev. 9-10; Ps. 50; Luke 14
20 Lev. 11-12; Ps. 51; Luke 15
21 Lev. 13; Ps. 52; Luke 16
22 Lev. 14; Ps. 53; Luke 17
23 Lev. 15-16; Ps. 54; Luke 18
24 Lev. 17-18; Ps. 55; Luke 19
25 Lev. 19-20; Ps. 56; Luke 20
26 Lev. 21-22; Ps. 57; Luke 21
27 Lev. 23-24; Ps. 58; Luke 22
28 Lev. 25
29 Ps. 59; Luke 23

MARCH

1 Lev. 26-27; Ps. 60; Luke 24
2 Num. 1-2; Ps. 61; John 1
3 Num. 3-4; Ps. 62; John 2-3
4 Num. 5-6; Ps. 63; John 4
5 Num. 7; Ps. 64; John 5
6 Num. 8-9; Ps. 65; John 6
7 Num. 10-11; Ps. 66; John 7
8 Num. 12-13; Ps. 67; John 8
9 Num. 14-15; Ps. 68; John 9
10 Num. 16; Ps. 69; John 10
11 Num. 17-18; Ps. 70; John 11
12 Num. 19-20; Ps. 71; John 12
13 Num. 21-22; Ps. 72; John 13
14 Num. 23-24; Ps. 73; John 14-15
15 Num. 25-26; Ps. 74; John 16
16 Num. 27-28; Ps. 75; John 17
17 Num. 29-30; Ps. 76; John 18
18 Num. 31-32; Ps. 77; John 19
19 Num. 23-24; Ps. 78; John 20
20 Num. 35-36; Ps. 79; John 21
21 Deut. 1-2; Ps. 80; Acts 1
22 Deut. 3-4; Ps. 81; Acts 2
23 Deut. 5-6; Ps. 82; Acts 3-4
24 Deut. 7-8; Ps. 83; Acts 5-6
25 Deut. 9-10; Ps. 84; Acts 7
26 Deut. 11-12; Ps. 85; Acts 8
27 Deut. 13-14; Ps. 86; Acts 9
28 Deut. 15-16; Ps. 87; Acts 10
29 Deut. 17-18; Ps. 88; Acts 11-12
30 Deut. 19-20; Ps. 89; Acts 13
31 Deut. 21-22; Ps. 90; Acts 14

APRIL

1 Deut. 23-24; Ps. 91; Acts 15
2 Deut. 25-27; Ps. 92; Acts 16
3 Deut. 28-29; Ps. 93; Acts 17
4 Deut. 30-31; Ps. 94; Acts 18
5 Deut. 32; Ps. 95; Acts 19
6 Deut. 33-34; Ps. 96; Acts 20
7 Josh. 1-2; Ps. 97; Acts 21
8 Josh. 3-4; Ps. 98; Acts 22
9 Josh. 5-6; Ps. 99; Acts 23
10 Josh. 7-8; Ps. 100; Acts 24-25
11 Josh. 9-10; Ps. 101; Acts 26
12 Josh. 11-12; Ps. 102; Acts 27
13 Josh. 13-14; Ps. 103; Acts 28
14 Josh. 15-16; Ps. 104; Rom. 1-2
15 Josh. 17-18; Ps. 105; Rom. 3-4
16 Josh. 19-20; Ps. 106; Rom. 5-6
17 Josh. 21-22; Ps. 107; Rom. 7-8
18 Josh. 23-24; Ps. 108; Rom. 9-10
19 Judg. 1-2; Ps. 109; Rom. 11-12
20 Judg. 3-4; Ps. 110; Rom. 13-14
21 Judg. 5-6; Ps. 111; Rom. 15-16
22 Judg. 7-8; Ps. 112; 1 Cor. 1-2
23 Judg. 9; Ps. 113; 1 Cor. 3-4
24 Judg. 10-11; Ps. 114; 1 Cor. 5-6
25 Judg. 12-13; Ps. 115; 1 Cor. 7
26 Judg. 14-15; Ps. 116; 1 Cor. 8-9
27 Judg. 16-17; Ps. 117; 1 Cor. 10
28 Judg. 18-19; Ps. 118; 1 Cor. 11
29 Judg. 20-21; Ps. 119:1-88; 1 Cor. 12
30 Ruth 1-4; Ps. 119-89-176; 1 Cor. 13

MAY

1	1 Sam. 1-2; Ps. 120; 1 Cor. 14
2	1 Sam. 3-4; Ps. 121; 1 Cor. 15
3	1 Sam. 5-6; Ps. 122; 1 Cor. 16
4	1 Sam. 7-8; Ps. 123; 2 Cor. 1
5	1 Sam. 9-10; Ps. 124; 2 Cor. 2-3
6	1 Sam. 11-12; Ps. 125; 2 Cor. 4-5
7	1 Sam. 13-14; Ps. 126; 2 Cor. 6-7
8	1 Sam. 15-16; Ps. 127; 2 Cor. 8
9	1 Sam. 17; Ps. 128; 2 Cor. 9-10
10	1 Sam. 18-19; Ps. 129; 2 Cor. 11
11	1 Sam. 20-21; Ps. 130; 2 Cor. 12
12	1 Sam. 22-23; Ps. 131; 2 Cor. 13
13	1 Sam. 24-25; Ps. 132; Gal. 1-2
14	1 Sam. 26-27; Ps. 133; Gal. 3-4
15	1 Sam. 28-29; Ps. 134; Gal. 5-6
16	1 Sam. 30-31; Ps. 135; Eph. 1-2
17	2 Sam. 1-2; Ps. 136;Eph. 3-4
18	2 Sam. 3-4; Ps. 137; Eph. 5-6
19	2 Sam. 5-6; Ps. 138; Phil. 1-2
20	2 Sam. 7-8; Ps. 139; Phil. 3-4
21	2 Sam. 9-10; Ps. 140; Col. 1-2
22	2 Sam. 11-12; Ps. 141; Col. 3-4
23	2 Sam. 13-14; Ps. 142; 1 Thess. 1-2
24	1 Sam. 15-16; Ps. 143; 1 Thess. 3-4
25	2 Sam. 17-18; Ps. 144; 1 Thess. 5
26	2 Sam. 19; Ps. 145; 2 Thess. 1-3
27	2 Sam. 20-21; Ps. 146; 1 Tim. 1-2
28	2 Sam. 22; Ps. 147; 1 Tim. 3-4
29	2 Sam. 23-24; Ps. 148; 1 Tim. 5-6
30	1 Kings 1; Ps. 149; 2 Tim. 1-2
31	1 Kings 2-3; Ps. 150; 2 Tim. 3-4

JUNE

1	1 Kings 4-5; Prov. 1; Titus 1-3
2	1 Kings 6-7; Prov. 2; Philem.
3	1 Kings 8; Prov. 3; Heb. 1-2
4	1 Kings 9-10; Prov. 4; Heb. 3-4
5	1 Kings 11-12; Prov. 5; Heb. 5-6
6	1 Kings 13-14; Prov. 6; Heb. 7-8
7	1 Kings 15-16; Prov. 7; Heb. 9-10
8	1 Kings 17-18; Prov. 8; Heb. 11
9	1 Kings 19-20; Prov. 9; Heb. 12
10	1 Kings 21-22; Prov. 10; Heb. 13
11	2 Kings 1-2; Prov. 11; James 1
12	2 Kings 3-4; Prov. 12; James 2-3
13	2 Kings 5-6; Prov. 13; James 4-5
14	2 Kings 7-8; Prov. 14; 1 Pet. 1
15	2 Kings 9-10; Prov. 15; 1 Pet. 2-3
16	2 Kings 11-12; Prov. 16; 1 Pet. 4-5
17	2 Kings 13-14; Prov. 17; 2 Pet. 1-3
18	2 Kings 15-16; Prov. 18; 1 John 1-2
19	2 Kings 17; Prov. 19; 1 John 3-4
20	2 Kings 18-19; Prov. 20; 1 John 5
21	2 Kings 20-21; Prov. 21; 2 John
22	2 Kings 22-23; Prov. 22; 3 John
23	2 Kings 24-25; Prov. 23; Jude
24	1 Chron. 1; Prov. 24; Rev. 1-2
25	1 Chron. 2-3; Prov. 25; Rev. 3-5
26	1 Chron. 4-5; Prov. 26; Rev. 6-7
27	1 Chron. 6-7; Prov. 27; Rev. 8-10
28	1 Chron. 8-9; Prov. 28; Rev. 11-12
29	1 Chron. 10-11; Prov. 29; Rev. 13-14
30	1 Chron. 12-13; Prov. 30; Rev. 15-17

JULY

1	1 Chron. 14-15; Prov. 31; Rev. 18-19
2	1 Chron. 16-17; Ps. 1; Rev. 20-22
3	1 Chron. 18-19; Ps. 2; Matt. 1-2
4	1 Chron. 20-21; Ps. 3; Matt. 3-4
5	1 Chron. 22-23; Ps. 4; Matt. 5
6	1 Chron. 24-25; Ps. 5; Matt. 6-7
7	1 Chron. 26-27; Ps. 6; Matt. 8-9
8	1 Chron. 28-29; Ps. 7; Matt. 10-11
9	2 Chron. 1-2; Ps. 8; Matt. 12
10	2 Chron. 3-4; Ps. 9; Matt. 13
11	2 Chron. 5-6; Ps. 10; Matt. 14-15
12	2 Chron. 7-8; Ps. 11; Matt. 16-17
13	2 Chron. 9-10; Ps. 12; Matt. 18
14	2 Chron. 11-12; Ps. 13; Matt. 19-20
15	2 Chron. 13-14; Ps. 14; Matt. 21
16	2 Chron. 15-16; Ps. 15; Matt. 22
17	2 Chron. 17-18; Ps. 16; Matt. 23
18	2 Chron. 19-20; Ps. 17; Matt. 24
19	2 Chron. 21-22; Ps. 18; Matt. 25
20	2 Chron. 23-24; Ps. 19; Matt. 26
21	2 Chron. 25-26; Ps. 20; Matt. 27
22	2 Chron. 27-28; Ps. 21; Matt. 28
23	2 Chron. 29-30; Ps. 22; Mark 1
24	2 Chron. 31-32; Ps. 23; Mark 2
25	2 Chron. 33-34; Ps. 24; Mark 3
26	2 Chron. 35-36; Ps. 25; Mark 4
27	Ezra 1-2; Ps. 26; Mark 5
28	Ezra 3-4; Ps. 27; Mark 6
29	Ezra 5-6; Ps. 28; Mark 7
30	Ezra 7-8; Ps. 29; Mark 8
31	Ezra 9-10; Ps. 30; Mark 9

AUGUST

1	Neh. 1-2; Ps. 31; Mark 10
2	Neh. 3-4; Ps. 32; Mark 11
3	Neh. 5-6; Ps. 33; Mark 12
4	Neh. 7; Ps. 34; Mark 13
5	Neh. 8-9; Ps. 35; Mark 14
6	Neh. 10-11; Ps. 36; Mark 15
7	Neh. 12-13; Ps. 37; Mark 16
8	Esth. 1-2; Ps. 38; Luke 1
9	Esth. 3-4; Ps. 39; Luke 2
10	Esth. 5-6; Ps. 40; Luke 3
11	Esth. 7-8; Ps. 41; Luke 4
12	Esth. 9-10; Ps. 42; Luke 5
13	Job 1-2; Ps. 43; Luke 6
14	Job 3-4; Ps. 44; Luke 7
15	Job 5-6; Ps. 45; Luke 8
16	Job 7-8; Ps. 46; Luke 9
17	Job 9-10; Ps. 47; Luke 10
18	Job 11-12; Ps. 48; Luke 11
19	Job 13-14; Ps. 49; Luke 12
20	Job 15-16; Ps. 50; Luke 13
21	Job. 17-18; Ps. 51; Luke 14
22	Job 19-20; Ps. 52; Luke 15
23	Job 21-22; Ps. 53; Luke 16
24	Job 23-25; Ps. 54; Luke 17
25	Job 26-28; Ps. 55; Luke 18
26	Job 29-30; Ps. 56; Luke 19
27	Job 31-32; Ps. 57; Luke 20
28	Job 33-34; Ps. 58; Luke 21
29	Job 35-36; Ps. 59; Luke 22
30	Job 37-38; Ps. 60; Luke 23
31	Job 39-40; Ps. 61; Luke 24

SEPTEMBER

1	Job 41-42; Ps. 62; John 1
2	Eccl. 1-2; Ps. 63; John 2-3
3	Eccl. 3-4; Ps. 64; John 4
4	Eccl. 5-6; Ps. 65; John 5
5	Eccl. 7-8; Ps. 66; John 6
6	Eccl. 9-10; Ps. 67; John 7
7	Eccl. 11-12; Ps. 68; John 8
8	Song. of Sol. 1-2; Ps. 69; John 9
9	Song of Sol. 3-4; Ps. 70; John 10
10	Song of Sol. 5-6; Ps. 71; John 11
11	Song of Sol. 7-8; Ps. 72; John 12
12	Isaiah 1-2; Ps. 73; John 13
13	Isaiah 3-5; Ps. 74; John 14-15
14	Isaiah 6-8; Ps. 75; John 16
15	Isaiah 9-10; Ps. 76; John 17
16	Isaiah 11-13; Ps. 77; John 18
17	Isaiah 14-15; Ps. 78; John 19
18	Isaiah 16-17; Ps. 79; John 20
19	Isaiah 18-19; Ps. 80; John 21
20	Isaiah 20-22; Ps. 81; Acts 1
21	Isaiah 23-24; Ps. 82; Acts 2
22	Isaiah 25-26; Ps. 83; Acts 3-4
23	Isaiah 27-28; Ps. 84; Acts 5-6
24	Isaiah 29-30; Ps. 85; Acts 7
25	Isaiah 31-32; Ps. 86; Acts 8
26	Isaiah 33-34; Ps. 87; Acts 9
27	Isaiah 35-36; Ps. 88; Acts 10
28	Isaiah 37-38; Ps. 89; Acts 11-12
29	Isaiah 39-40; Ps. 90; Acts 13
30	Isaiah 41-42; Ps. 91; Acts 14

OCTOBER

1	Isaiah 43-44; Ps. 92; Acts 15
2	Isaiah 45-46; Ps. 93; Acts 16
3	Isaiah 47-48; Ps. 94; Acts 17
4	Isaiah 49-50; Ps. 95; Acts 18
5	Isaiah 51-52; Ps. 96; Acts 19
6	Isaiah 53-54; Ps. 97; Acts 20
7	Isaiah 55-56; Ps. 98; Acts 21
8	Isaiah 57-58; Ps. 99; Acts 22
9	Isaiah 59-60; Ps. 100; Acts 23
10	Isaiah 61-62; Ps. 101; Acts 24-25
11	Isaiah 63-64; Ps. 102; Acts 26
12	Isaiah 65-66; Ps. 103; Acts 27
13	Jer. 1-2; Ps. 104; Acts 28
14	Jer. 3-4; Ps. 105; Rom. 1-2
15	Jer. 5-6; Ps. 106; Rom. 3-4
16	Jer. 7-8; Ps. 107; Rom. 5-6
17	Jer. 9-10; Ps. 108; Rom. 7-8
18	Jer. 11-12; Ps. 109; Rom. 9-10
19	Jer. 13-14; Ps. 110; Rom. 11-12
20	Jer. 15-16; Ps. 111; Rom. 13-14
21	Jer. 17-18; Ps. 112; Rom. 15-16
22	Jer. 19-20; Ps. 113; 1 Cor. 1-2
23	Jer. 21-22; Ps. 114; 1 Cor. 3-4
24	Jer. 23-24; Ps. 115; 1 Cor. 5-6
25	Jer. 25-26; Ps. 116; 1 Cor. 7
26	Jer. 27-28; Ps. 117; 1 Cor. 8-9
27	Jer. 29-30; Ps. 118; 1 Cor. 10
28	Jer. 31-32; Ps. 119:1-64; 1 Cor. 11
29	Jer. 33-34; Ps. 119:65-120; 1 Cor. 12
30	Jer. 35-36; Ps. 119:121-176; 1 Cor. 13
31	Jer. 37-38; Ps. 120; 1 Cor. 14

NOVEMBER

1 Jer. 39-40; Ps. 121; 1 Cor. 15
2 Jer. 41-42; Ps. 122; 1 Cor. 16
3 Jer. 43-44; Ps. 123; 2 Cor. 1
4 Jer. 45-46; Ps. 124; 2 Cor. 2-3
5 Jer. 47-48; Ps. 125; 2 Cor. 4-5
6 Jer. 49-50; Ps. 126; 2 Cor. 6-7
7 Jer. 51-52; Ps. 127; 2 Cor. 8
8 Lam. 1-2; Ps. 128; 1 Cor. 9-10
9 Lam. 3; Ps. 129; 2 Cor. 11
10 Lam. 4-5; Ps. 130; 2 Cor. 12
11 Ezek. 1-2; Ps. 131; 2 Cor. 13
12 Ezek. 3-4; Ps. 132; Gal. 1-2
13 Ezek. 5-6; Ps. 133; Gal. 3-4
14 Ezek. 7-8; Ps. 134; Gal. 5-6
15 Ezek. 9-10; Ps. 135; Eph. 1-2
16 Ezek. 11-12; Ps. 136; Eph. 3-4
17 Ezek. 13-14; Ps. 137; Eph. 5-6
18 Ezek. 15-16; Ps. 138; Phil. 1-2
19 Ezek. 17-18; Ps. 139; Phil. 3-4
20 Ezek. 19-20; Ps. 140; Col. 1-2
21 Ezek. 21-22; Ps. 141; Col. 3-4
22 Ezek. 23-24; Ps. 142;
   1 Thess. 1-2
23 Ezek. 25-26; Ps. 143;
   1 Thess. 3-4
24 Ezek. 27-28; Ps. 144; 1 Thess. 5
25 Ezek. 29-30; Ps. 145;
   2 Thess. 1-3
26 Ezek. 31-32; Ps. 146; 1 Tim. 1-2
27 Ezek. 33-34; Ps. 147; 1 Tim. 3-4
28 Ezek. 35-36; Ps. 148; 1 Tim. 5-6
29 Ezek. 37-38; Ps. 149; 2 Tim. 1-2
30 Ezek. 39-40; Ps. 150; 2 Tim. 3-4

DECEMBER

1 Ezek. 41-42; Prov. 1; Titus 1-3
2 Ezek. 43-44; Prov. 2; Philem.
3 Ezek. 45-46; Prov. 3; Heb 1-2
4 Ezek. 47-48; Prov. 4; Heb. 3-4
5 Dan. 1-2; Prov. 5; Heb. 5-6
6 Dan. 3-4; Prov. 6; Heb. 7-8
7 Dan. 5-6; Prov. 7; Heb. 9-10
8 Dan. 7-8; Prov. 8; Heb. 11
9 Dan. 9-10; Prov. 9; Heb. 12
10 Dan. 11-12; Prov. 10; Heb. 13
11 Hos. 1-3; Prov. 11; James 1-3
12 Hos. 4-6; Prov. 12; James 4-5
13 Hos. 7-8; Prov. 13; 1 Pet. 1
14 Hos. 9-11; Prov. 14; 1 Pet. 2-3
15 Hos. 12-14; Prov. 15; 1 Pet. 4-5
16 Joel 1-3; Prov. 16; 2 Pet. 1-3
17 Amos 1-3; Prov. 17; 1 John 1-2
18 Amos 4-6; Prov. 18; 1 John 3-4
19 Amos 7-9; Prov. 19; 1 John 5
20 Obad.; Prov. 20; 2 John
21 Jonah 1-4; Prov. 21; 3 John
22 Mic. 1-4; Prov. 22; Jude
23 Mic. 5-7; Prov. 23; Rev. 1-2
24 Nah. 1-3; Prov. 24; Rev. 3-5
25 Hab. 1-3; Prov. 25; Rev. 6-7
26 Zeph. 1-3; Prov. 26; Rev. 8-10
27 Hag. 1-2; Prov. 27; Rev. 11-12
28 Zech. 1-4; Prov. 28; Rev. 13-14
29 Zech. 5-9; Prov. 29; Rev. 15-17
30 Zech. 10-14; Prov. 30; Rev. 18-19
31 Mal. 1-4; Prov. 31; Rev. 20-22

Recommended Reading

Communication, Sex and Money, Edwin Louis Cole, Harrison House.

From Faith to Faith — A Daily Guide to Victory, Kenneth & Gloria Copeland, Distributed by Harrison House.

The Making of a Man, Richard Exley, Honor Books, Tulsa, Oklahoma.

One Flesh, Bob Yandian, Distributed by Harrison House.

Courtship After Marriage, Zig Ziglar, Oliver Nelson Publishers, Nashville, Tennessee.

Building Stronger Marriages and Families, Billy Joe Daugherty, Harrison House.

Prayers That Avail Much for Fathers, Word Ministries, Harrison House.

The Father's Topical Bible, Honor Books, Tulsa, Oklahoma.

Ministering to Your Family, Kenneth E. Hagin, Kenneth Hagin Ministries, Tulsa, Oklahoma.

Maximized Manhood, Edwin Louis Cole, Whitaker House Publishers, Springdale, Pennsylvania.

Bibliography

Avanzini, John. "God Wants You To Prosper," *Always Abounding – The Way To Prosper in Good Times, Bad Times, Any Time*. Tulsa: Harrison House, 1989, pp. 117-122.

Cole, Edwin Louis. "God Made Sex Good," *Communication, Sex and Money*. Tulsa: Harrison House, 1987, pp. 97-104.

Copeland, Kenneth. "Honoring God on Your Job," *Honor – Walking in Honesty, Truth and Integrity*. Tulsa: Harrison House, 1992, pp. 86-96.

Copeland, Kenneth & Gloria. "Heaven on Earth in Your Home and Marriage," *Believer's Voice of Victory*. Vol. 15, No. 12, 1987, pp. 9,10.

Daugherty, Billy Joe. "Men Taking the Spiritual Leadership in the Home," *Building Stronger Marriages and Families*. Tulsa: Harrison House, 1991, pp. 121,122.

Exley, Richard. "The Making of a Family," *Building Relationships That Last – Life's Bottom Line*. Tulsa: Honor Books, 1990, pp. 209-220.

Price, Frederick K. C. "The Duties of a Husband: Love Your Wife as Yourself," *Marriage & the Family*. Tulsa: Harrison House, 1988, pp. 75-88,304.